FLOWERS

A GUIDE TO ANNUALS, PERENNIALS, FLOWER ARRANGEMENTS, AND MORE!

pil

Publications International, Ltd.

Photography by Christopher Hiltz

Additional images from Shutterstock.com and Wikimedia Commons.

Flower arrangements by Lorraine Rudin

Louis Weber, CEO
Publications International, Ltd.
8140 Lehigh Avenue
Morton Grove, IL 60053

ISBN: 978-1-64558-122-2

Manufactured in China.

8 7 6 5 4 3 2 1

Table of Contents

Chapter 1
ANNUALS 6

Chapter 2
PERENNIALS. 16

Chapter 3
GROWING YOUR OWN FLOWERS 28

Chapter 4
PLANT PROFILES 50

Chapter 5
FLOWER ARRANGING 110

INTRODUCTION

Flowers are more than beautiful gifts of nature. They are essential to life itself. Their importance to humanity is most obvious in the food chain. In the forms of broccoli, cauliflower, and artichokes, for example, flowers are themselves food for humans; farther on down the food chain flowers feed the creatures that in turn feed humans. Through the ages people have used flowers to make medicines that eased pain and healed wounds. Today we value flowers for their beauty, fragrance, and symbolism. We use flowers to adorn ourselves, decorate spaces, mark special occasions, and give as gifts.

This book is designed to enhance your enjoyment of flowers. You'll learn about annuals and perennials, how to care for them, and how to arrange them in stunning works of floral art.

Chapter 1 is all about annuals. You'll learn about the various types of annuals, how to use annuals in your home and garden, what characteristics to look for when selecting annuals, and how to care for them.

Chapter 2 explores perennials in detail. Learn about all the different types of perennials, their many uses, qualities to look for in perennials, and how best to care for them.

Chapter 3 delves into how to grow your own flower garden. You'll get practical advice on planning a garden based on your unique site conditions, deciding what to plant, color considerations, installing flowers, and how to care for your garden once it's planted.

Chapter 4 is a colorful directory of more than 85 popular plants. The entries include common and botanical names, descriptions, growing techniques, suggested uses, and related species and varieties. Color photographs are included for each plant profiled.

Chapter 5 provides a primer on flower arranging. You'll learn about the supplies you'll need, how to condition flowers, basic design principles, and how to make 11 different flower arrangements from start to finish.

Annuals: These germinate, bloom, set seed, and die all in one year. Examples include bachelor's buttons, marigolds, and zinnias.

Biennials: These complete their life cycle in two years, producing foliage the first year and flowers the second. Examples include foxglove and hollyhock.

Perennials: These live for two or more years, getting bigger and better each year. Examples include basket-of-gold, peonies, and daylilies.

Bulbs: These are plants with fleshy underground structures. They include true bulbs, such as daffodils, and plants with fleshy roots and stems, such as dahlias and tuberous begonias.

Chapter 1

ANNUALS

What Are Annuals?

Annuals are fun and flamboyant flowering and foliage plants that germinate, grow, flower, produce seed, and die—all within a single growing season. Like thoroughbreds at the racetrack, they're off to a quick start—flowering in as little as six or eight weeks after the seed germinates and providing instant color when you buy plants pre-started in a greenhouse. Their fast-paced lifestyle provides welcome contrast to trees, which may take decades to mature, and even to young perennials, which may take a couple years to fill out.

Unlike hardy perennials and trees, however, annuals are transient. It is their nature to die when their life cycle is finished or when frost and winter cold cut their existence short. This opens up an endless choice of new options for you. Using fresh, new plants each spring, you can change past color schemes, height arrangements, and even subtle combinations of leaf texture.

While these generalizations provide a good working definition of annuals, the huge cast of characters we call annuals encompasses a potpourri of different kinds of performers.

True annuals in the botanical sense live only one growing season, or even less time. Their life span is genetically programmed to end after they have flowered and set seed, paving the way for a new generation of plants. Sweet alyssum, for example, which thrives in cool spring temperatures, produces tiny, white, sweet-scented flowers in abundance. But the combination of summer's heat and the stress of seed production often finishes the plant. This is not a sad story, because when the cool, moist weather of late summer or fall arrives, seeds dropped by that first plant may sprout into another generation.

Tender perennials, which account for most of the bedding annuals we grow, include geraniums, impatiens, begonias, and ornamental peppers. They are quick-maturing tropical or subtropical plants that thrive during warm weather but die with the first heavy autumn frost. If brought indoors before this chilly final curtain, pots of geraniums, fuchsias, perillas, hibiscus, and others could continue to grow for many years.

CLASSIFYING ANNUALS

Annuals can be classified as hardy, half-hardy, or tender based on their tolerance of cold temperatures.

Hardy Annuals: Hardy annuals such as sweet alyssum, calendula, and bachelor's button grow best in cool weather and can withstand some frost and freezing. These are often planted outdoors as soon as the soil can be worked in spring.

Bachelor's button (*Centaurea cyanus*), also known as cornflower, is a hardy annual.

Gazania (*Gazania rigens*), also called treasure flower, is a half-hardy annual.

Tender Annuals: Tender annuals such as zinnia and cockscomb are sensitive to cold. In most areas, these plants are started indoors and transplanted outdoors after the frost free date, when the soil is warm.

Zinnia (*Zinnia elegans*) is a tender annual.

Half-Hardy Annuals: Half-hardy annuals can tolerate cool weather but are damaged by repeated exposure to frost. These plants are often started early indoors and planted outdoors when the danger of prolonged frost is past. Examples include petunia and gazania.

When it comes to versatility, annuals are champs. They are fast performers, speedier than any other type of plant, providing nearly instant results in any garden.

Annuals' finite, one-season-long life cycle also has advantages. If you move, you won't be reluctant to leave the annual garden behind. You can replant annuals wherever you go just as easily as you did before. This is perfect for renters, who can enjoy one bright growing season without worrying about what will happen next year.

Annuals don't need any elaborate staging. You don't even have to own a house and yard or dig in the dirt at all. Many annuals will thrive in commercial planting mixes in pots or planters on a patio or balcony. They grow without worry for winter survival—as there would be for perennials—or any need for complex sheltering and wintering schemes.

CHARACTERISTICS OF EASY-CARE ANNUALS

For the past several decades, most large seed companies have focused on developing annuals that would inspire winter-weary gardeners making spring shopping trips. They developed neat, compact, early-blooming varieties that caught the eye in a 6-pack or 4-inch pot. But it didn't take long before annual suppliers realized that presenting a pretty package in the garden center wasn't enough. People want annuals that are going to perform well in the garden long after they leave the store. Consequently, they've endowed some of the easiest-growing annual varieties with improved resistance to diseases, a naturally full form, cold and heat tolerance, and sturdy, non-flopping stems. It is wise to look for some of these qualities in annuals for your garden.

The hybrid zinnia Profusion series is a disease-resistant high performer.

Disease Resistance: For an annual to provide you with outstanding performance, it has to be healthy. There is no easier or better way to ensure good health than to plant annuals that are naturally immune to problem diseases.

Garden zinnias (*Zinnia elegans*), although enthusiastic bloomers and high performers, are particularly prone to powdery mildew which attacks during warm, humid weather, coating the plant with ugly white pallor and causing the flowers and leaves to drop. In contrast, closely related *Zinnia angustifolia*, which develops smaller marigold-like flowers, is immune to powdery mildew. Hybrids between these two species, such as the Profusion series, combine the flashy flowers of garden zinnias with built-in disease tolerance from *Zinnia angustifolia*—effectively achieving the best of both worlds.

Look for heat-tolerant cultivars of ivy geraniums (*Pelargonium peltatum*).

Heat and Cold Tolerance: One of the true tests of an easy-care annual comes when mild spring weather turns to the blazing heat of summer. This inevitable change can spell the end to annuals that cannot tolerate too much heat. If heat tolerance is a priority in your area, look for annuals such as melampodium, native to Mexico and Central America, that are natural heat-lovers. Or for annuals like ivy geraniums, that ordinarily suffer in hot weather, look for heat-tolerant cultivars such as 'Matador Burgundy' and 'Matador Light Pink.'

Likewise, the transition from warm, frost-free weather in fall to frosty, late autumn weather finishes off most annuals. But a few hardy annuals, such as pansies, take the change without faltering. 'Maxim Marina' is one of the most exceptionally cold-tolerant pansy cultivars. It usually even opens a few blooms in late winter whenever the snow melts—a pleasant harbinger of spring.

Self-Branching: Your mother's handsome bed of annuals may have been achieved only with painstaking pinching, removing the tip of every main stem on every plant. This process slows upward growth and encourages side branch development. It transforms a naturally tall and lanky plant into a full and bushy shape with more abundant blossoms. Thankfully, most modern types of impatiens, begonias (*below*), multiflora petunias, and other annuals have been bred to be self-branching. They stay fuller naturally and may not need any pinching, or at least very little.

Naturally Compact Growth: Neat, low-growing annuals have been a hot commodity, primarily because they look great in the spring nursery. They also need little planning to use in the garden as they can spread in low sweeps across the front of a garden, below shrubs and trees, and in large, bright, ground-hugging bedding schemes. If you like annuals to be low, you have an excellent selection from which to choose. Melampodium (*above*), for instance, reaches only 10 to 15 inches in height and spreads even wider to make a graceful, low mound. Sunflowers, gangly annuals reaching heights as grand as 10 feet, have been reduced to knee-height with the cultivar 'Sun Spot.' And this strain bears full-sized flower heads regardless of its miniature stem.

Self-Supporting Stems and Flowers: Not everyone wants compact flowers. Long-legged flowers work well for providing height in the rear of the annual garden, filling in the gaps between newly planted perennials, or providing long-stemmed cut flowers. However, in order to qualify as an easy-growing annual, long-stemmed beauties must be sturdy enough to hold their own flowers up and not fall flat in a gale.

One of the best of the tall annuals is the stately canna (*left*), a tender perennial that has a stocky main stem that may reach a height of 5 feet and bear large tropical leaves and spikes of big, bright flowers. For a sturdy-stemmed, 18-inch-tall version of the compact ageratum, with its charming blue, powder-puff flowers, look for 'Blue Horizon.' There are also taller and easy-growing versions of begonias, marigolds, and calendulas well worth considering.

Self-Shedding Flowers: A few annuals, such as Shirley and California poppies, are self-shedding. They drop their old petals naturally so you don't have to watch them deteriorate or go outside and cut them off. You may want to remove the developing seed pods, however, so plants can put their energy back into producing more flowers and maintaining their foliage.

Shirley and California poppies are self-shedding annuals.

MAKING YOUR ANNUALS AT HOME

Most annuals, with the exception of certain fussy rare wildflowers and unusual alpines, can be easy to grow if you keep one condition in mind. You need to find annuals that will thrive in the growing conditions—sun or shade and soil type—you have at home.

Manhandling even the most durable petunia into a deeply shaded, root-riddled nook under a large spruce tree won't produce satisfactory results. Where conditions are marginal, annuals seldom grow or flower and, in this weakened state, fall prey to pests and diseases. But put the same plant into loose, rich, and fertile soil and full sun, and it can reward you with lavish blossoms for months.

Read Chapter 3 to learn about your site conditions. Then pay attention to the labels on annuals in garden centers and consult details in Chapter 4 to find a plant that matches your garden's quotient of sun or shade, light or heavy soil. Where you have full sun, globe amaranth and cosmos are ideal. For well-drained, light soil, try candytuft and lantana. Where the soil stays moist most of the time, caladiums, calla lilies, and fuchsias thrive.

Certain extra-easy annuals, such as fibrous-rooted begonias and ageratums, are flexible and adaptable. They can grow in a variety of good garden sites in sun or light shade. Coleus, with rainbow-colored leaves, stays more compact in full sun and needs careful attention to watering. But it also thrives in shade, reaching slightly greater heights and often going for longer periods without extra irrigation. Beginning gardeners, still getting a feel for site conditions, can get great results when working with these easy-growing annuals.

CARING FOR YOUR ANNUALS

Annuals will flourish when provided with the best growing conditions. However, there are a few simple care techniques you can employ to help keep your annuals happy and healthy.

Watering: Annuals require regular watering throughout their short lives. Test soil moisture by poking your finger 2 to 3 inches into the ground to feel how moist or dry it is. Taking a pinch from the surface isn't good enough; you need to know what conditions are like down in the root zone. When you do need to water, always water deeply. Surface soil dries out more rapidly than deeper soil, and when it does, shallow-rooted plants quickly wilt. Whenever you water, check to see that the water has seeped down to a depth of 6 to 8 inches by sticking your finger down into the soil. Using a soaker hose will minimize waste due to runoff and evaporation.

Fertilize Annuals Periodically: Fertilize annuals periodically during the growing season to keep them producing. This is particularly helpful after the first flush of blooming flowers begins to fade (which often marks the beginning of a quiet garden during hot summer months). For best results, deadhead, then fertilize with a balanced water-soluble or granular fertilizer. A balanced fertilizer contains similar percentages of nitrogen, phosphorus, and potassium. Follow package instructions when applying fertilizer.

Pinching and Shearing: Pinching and shearing are grooming techniques that encourage plants to branch out and grow fuller. Shearing consists of using a sharp-bladed implement to cut back the entire top of a plant by several inches. This encourages the plant to send out, and direct energy to, more side branches. Pinching involves removing just the last inch or so of the main growing tip, usually with your fingers. This will redirect the plant's energy from a single shoot to numerous latent side buds (a latent growth bud is located at each node, which is the point on the stem where a leaf is attached). Several days after pinching, you'll see several small shoots pushing out from the remaining stem. These will grow into a cluster of stems to replace the original single stem. The result will be a shorter, stockier, fuller plant that looks neater and has more branches on which to produce flowers.

Deadheading: Remove spent blossoms from geraniums and other annuals to keep them blooming and tidy. The bigger the flower, the worse it can look when faded, brown, and mushy. Large, globular geranium flowers are particularly prominent when they begin to discolor. Snip off the entire flower cluster. Take off the stem, too, if no other flower buds are waiting to bloom. This process is called deadheading.

Deadheading should be done soon after the flower dies, so no plant energy is wasted on seed formation. Single flowers should be cut back to the place on the stem where a side shoot is already pushing out. If none is evident, then cut back to above a leaf, a node, or a side branch. Cluster flowers will look fresh and attractive longer if the individual florets are snapped out of the group as they die.

Chapter 2

PERENNIALS

What Are Perennials?

Perennials are a varied group of long-lived plants that provide years of color and gardening pleasure. One of the key differences between perennials and annuals is that perennials survive winter outdoors, then produce new growth and flowers the following season. Annuals, on the other hand, germinate, grow, flower, produce seed, and die in a single season. Annuals must be planted every year while perennials are more or less permanent in the garden after they have been planted.

Another distinguishing characteristic of perennials is that most of them are herbaceous. Simply put, an herbaceous plant is a nonwoody plant that dies to the ground each year and reemerges the following season from growth points below the soil. Peonies, irises, and daylilies are well-known examples of herbaceous perennials. There are also a few evergreen perennials, such as Cheddar pinks (*Dianthus gratianopolitanus*), Japanese spurge (*Pachysandra terminalis*), and Lenten rose (*Helleborus orientalis*), that survive winter above ground with green leaves.

Unlike annuals that flower continuously for several months, most perennials only bloom for a few weeks. However, if you plan your garden with careful attention to ease of care, bloom sequence, handsome foliage, and winter interest, you can enjoy a perennial garden that will be in bloom for many months. Perennial gardens are intriguing because they never stay quite the same. Daily walks through the garden are filled with surprises as new plants come into bloom in ever-changing colors.

You will find that your perennial garden changes from year to year, especially during the first few years. A newly planted perennial garden looks pretty spare compared to the exuberance of a mature, three- or four-year-old garden. And there is always the chance that you will add and subtract plants over the years or rearrange plants to emphasize particular color or texture combinations.

Both new and seasoned gardeners can be rewarded with dependable beauty and many enjoyable hours in the garden by selecting reliable, easy perennials and matching them to their proper growing conditions.

Left: English garden with an herbaceous flower border

While most perennials share the common characteristic of persisting in the garden year after year, there is a great deal of variation among different species in terms of life span, flowering season, heat tolerance, winter hardiness, and ultimate size. One key to growing perennials successfully is knowing something about the individual characteristics of the plants you choose. If you know what to expect from a particular plant, then you are more likely to place it in the proper location and give it the kind of care that encourages healthy, vigorous growth.

Longevity or life span is one characteristic that varies greatly among perennials. Some perennials, such as peonies and hostas, are very long-lived with plants easily living 20 years or more. Other long-lived perennials include astilbes, moss phlox (*Phlox subulata*), ferns, heartleaf bergenia (*Bergenia cordifolia*), Lenten rose (*Helleborus orientalis*), different kinds of sedum, and Solomon's seal (*Polygonatum* species).

Peonies (*Paeonia* species) are very long-lived perennials that can live up to 100 years or more.

Foxglove is a biennial.

Some perennials, such as columbine (*Aquilegia* species) and Shasta daisy (*Leucanthemum x superbum*), are decidedly less permanent. In the case of columbine, the original plant (also called the mother plant), sets seed and then dies. Then new seedlings emerge and replace the original plant. However, the seedlings of hybrid plants seldom look like the parent plant; that's why the blue columbine you may have originally planted might come back in different colors, such as red or yellow. Many varieties of Shasta daisy bloom vigorously the first year, then become weak or die out the following season. These plants are said to "bloom themselves to death." Once you understand this, it's easy to keep fresh daisies going year after year by dividing the original plant and replanting the new divisions every two years. (For more on dividing perennials, see page 46.)

Although they are usually sold as perennials, plants such as foxglove (*Digitalis purpurea*), hollyhock (*Alcea rosea*), and sweet william (*Dianthus barbatus*), are really better classified as biennials. Biennials are plants that complete their life cycle in two growing seasons. They generally produce leaves the first year but not flowers. In the second year, they flower, set seed, and die. Once again, if you know which plants fit this growth pattern you will know how to keep these plants as permanent garden residents. Just let them set seed and allow new seedlings to take the place of the original plants.

Perennials also differ from one another in terms of how many times they bloom each growing season. Some plants are genetically programmed to bloom only once per season, so no amount of coaxing will get them to bloom again. Some perennials that exhibit this trait are astilbe (*Astilbe x arendsii*), bear's breeches (*Acanthus spinosus*), blue starflower (*Amsonia tabernaemontana*), goat's beard (*Aruncus dioicus*), Joe Pye weed (*Eupatorium maculatum*), and peony (*Paeonia* hybrids).

Repeat-blooming perennials, such as coreopsis, purple coneflower (*Echinacea purpurea*), pincushion flower (*Scabiosa columbaria*), Shasta daisy (*Leucanthemum x superbum*), tall phlox (*Phlox paniculata*), valerian (*Centranthus ruber*), and yarrow (*Achillea* species), can bloom for many weeks—and even months—if the old flowers are deadheaded. Deadheading refers to pruning faded flowers from a plant. When designing with long-blooming plants like these, you generally want to consider flower color and form over foliage.

There are a few spring-blooming perennials referred to as ephemerals. Ephemerals are perennials that go dormant after flowering and dispersing seed. Spring-blooming woodland wildflowers, such as Dutchman's breeches (*Dicentra cucullaria*), Virginia bluebells (*Mertensia virginica*), and wake robin (*Trillium* species), are all garden-worthy plants when used in a woodland garden for spring interest.

Dutchman's breeches (*Dicentra cucullaria*) is a perennial herbaceous plant that blooms in the early spring from March to April. The common name derives from their white flowers that resemble breeches.

USING PERENNIALS IN THE GARDEN

Perennials can be used in many different ways in the garden. Ornamental grasses and brightly blooming flowers, such as purple coneflower (*Echinacea purpurea*), black-eyed Susan (*Rudbeckia hirta*), and goldenrod (*Solidago*), can be grown in bold masses in what is now known as the "new American garden style." Perennials can be mixed with smaller trees, flowering shrubs, evergreens, vines, and bulbs in a layered garden. Perennials and annuals happily coexist in the abundance of loosely arranged cottage gardens. Perennials can also cover the ground under a tree or hold a slope that is too steep to mow. They can be grown in containers and used to mark an entryway, to brighten an outdoor entertaining area, or to mask a bare spot in the garden. For the most part, the varied uses for perennials are as wide as your imagination.

CUT FLOWERS

Many perennials make excellent cut flowers. If you enjoy bringing fresh flowers indoors, but hesitate to cut them from your regular gardens, consider setting aside a cutting garden. Find a spot that receives at least a half a day of sun and that has reasonably good soil. You might want to locate your cut-flower garden in an out-of-the-way spot where you won't notice the missing blooms. Feel free to use both annuals and perennials in your cut-flower garden.

PERENNIALS FOR A CUT-FLOWER GARDEN

Aster (*Aster* species)

Black-eyed Susan (*Rudbeckia hirta*)

Foxglove (*Digitalis purpurea*)

Coreopsis (*Coreopsis* species)

Feverfew (*Tanacetum parthenium*)

Blanket flower (*Gaillardia × grandiflora*)

Blazingstar (*Liatris* species)

Heliopsis (*Heliopsis* species)

Pincushion flower (*Scabiosa caucasica*)

Peony (*Paeonia* species)

Lupine (*Lupinus* species)

Hollyhock (*Alcea rosea*)

Goldenrod (*Solidago* species)

Yarrow (*Achillea* species)

Sweet william (*Dianthus barbatus*)

Purple coneflower (*Echinacea purpurea*)

Siberian iris (*Iris sibirica*)

Poppy (*Papaver* species)

Shasta daisy (*Leucanthemum × superbum*)

Valerian (*Valeriana officinalis*)

Qualities of Easy-Care Perennials

There are a number of traits that currently distinguish easy-care perennials. For a perennial to perform well in the garden it must be resistant to diseases and tolerant of pests that commonly afflict plants in your region. For example, powdery mildew is a fungal disease that attacks two perennial garden favorites: bee balm (*Monarda* species) and garden phlox (*Phlox paniculata*). Both of these plants are hit hard during warm weather by this dis-figuring disease, which coats plants with an ugly white pallor and causes leaves to drop. Fortunately, several highly mildew-resistant bee balm cultivars and phlox varieties have been introduced.

Another indicator of an easy-care perennial is heat and cold tolerance. If heat tolerance is an issue where you garden, look for perennials that thrive in warm climates, such as sunset hyssop (*Agastache rupestris*) and gray santolina (*Santolina chamaecyparissus*). If you live where summers are cool, look for perennials that enjoy those conditions, such as lupines (*Lupinus* hybrids) and monkshood (*Aconitum* species).

Above: Lupines thrive in places with cool summers.

Perennials with self-supporting stems and flowers also help keep garden care easy. One perennial that is notorious for flopping (falling over) is the peony. Many gardeners avoid peonies because they've sadly seen flower heads bend to the ground after a heavy rain. Fortunately you can still grow easy-care peonies by selecting varieties that don't flop because they have fewer flower petals, such as single, Japanese/anemone, and semi-double forms.

Repeat bloom is another valuable quality in easy-care perennials. After all, if a plant is occupying limited garden space, it's nice if it blooms for more than two weeks during the year. Many perennials will bloom for a minimum of four to six weeks if you deadhead them on a weekly basis. Good repeat bloomers are yarrow (*Achillea* species) and Shasta daisy (*Leucanthemum x superbum*).

Yarrow (*Achillea* species) can bloom for weeks and even months if the old flowers are deadheaded.

And finally, look for perennials that have clean foliage through most of the growing season. The leaves of some perennials turn brown and dry up after they flower. A few plants that have good-looking leaves when they are not flowering include hosta (*Hosta* species), barrenwort (*Epimedium* species), the yellow-flowered blackberry lily (*Belamcanda flabellata* 'Hello Yellow'), and coralbells (*Heuchera* species).

Once you have a solid understanding of the general differences in perennials, how they can be used, and what to look for in easy-care plants, you can move on to planning a new garden or updating an existing garden, as we will do in Chapter 3, Growing Your Own Flowers.

THREE TENETS OF EASY-CARE PERENNIAL GARDENING

Growing beautiful, colorful perennials is an easy and enjoyable undertaking if you keep three simple tenets in mind.

1. Soil preparation is everything. Soil is the natural element most critical to gardening success. It supports and feeds plants and provides water and oxygen to roots. Loose, friable (crumbly) soil is a joy to work with. No amount of additional water, fertilizer, or plant coddling produces the same positive results as does thorough soil preparation.

2. Put the right plant in the right place. As we said earlier in this chapter, not all perennials are created equal. Some perennials need at least seven hours of full sun to bloom while other perennials prefer afternoon shade. Still other plants need shade most of the day. Drought-tolerant perennials thrive in

soil that dries out thoroughly while other perennials need a constant supply of moisture to their roots. Many of the native prairie plants we use in our gardens grow quite happily in average, clay-laden garden soil while woodland species need rich soil with plenty of organic matter. You can save yourself a lot of grief, money, and work by matching the right plant to the right growing environment. Make sure you take time to get to know the light, moisture, soil, and wind conditions in your garden.

Remember, too, that it's perfectly acceptable to move plants that aren't happy. If you find that some of your daylilies refuse to bloom because they receive too much shade, don't hesitate to dig them out and move them to a sunnier location. Likewise, if your Joe Pye weed grown in full sun wilts and turns crispy, move it to a spot with afternoon shade and moister soil.

3. "Low maintenance" is not the same as "no maintenance." Thoughtfully selected, easy-to-grow perennials planted in properly prepared soil should not require intense care after they are established. But there is a difference between moderate care and no care; you can't turn your back on a perennial garden for a month at a time and expect it to look good. Most perennial gardens require some weeding, watering, and plant grooming (removing brown foliage or spent flowers). These tasks are pleasurable and manageable if done once a week.

Chapter 3

GROWING YOUR OWN FLOWERS

Planning Your Garden

If you've always dreamed of having a beautiful flower garden filled with colorful, thriving plants, but you didn't know quite where to start, get ready. This chapter makes that dream possible.

The best place to start the design process is by deciding what kind of garden you want, and where

you should plant it. Would you like a small flower bed in the backyard or by the front door? Or are you picturing a larger garden surrounding your terrace that includes patio containers or several flower beds? Starting small is certainly best. You can always enlarge a garden later.

KNOW YOUR SITE

Take time to analyze your growing conditions before you create a design or buy plants. No plant looks good if it's suffering. Although you can sometimes alter growing conditions, the best approach is to know what conditions your site offers and then to look for plants that will thrive in those conditions.

Sun and Shade

Watch how sunlight and shadows play over your yard to determine how much light a site receives before you create a design or select plants for that site. Gardeners and garden centers use the following terms to describe amounts of sun and shade:

FULL SUN. Sites that receive six to eight hours of direct sun a day are in full sun.

LIGHT SHADE. Sites that are shaded for part of the day but in direct sun for a good portion of it are located in light shade. You'll find light-shade sites under mature trees, because the sun can shine directly onto the ground beneath their high leaf canopy.

PARTIAL SHADE. Filtered light, or partial shade, can be found under trees that allow sunlight to penetrate through the canopy and dapple the ground throughout the day.

DEEP SHADE. Full, or deep, shade is the most difficult lighting condition. It is found under thickly branched trees or evergreens. A garden located in deep shade receives little or no direct sun. You might, however, be able to remove some lower branches from trees, thin out overcrowded branches in the canopy, or remove smaller scraggly or unwanted saplings and brush to brighten a densely shaded spot.

For a successful garden, stick to flowers that will thrive in the amount of sun or shade your site receives.

PLANTS FOR SHADE

You'll find more options once you start shopping, but this list will get you started.
- **PERENNIALS:** Hostas, ferns, hellebores, astilbes, epimediums, daylilies, hardy geraniums
- **ANNUALS:** Browallia, impatiens, begonias, coleus, alyssum, torenia, violas
- **BULBS:** Caladiums, tuberous begonias. Daffodils and other early blooming spring bulbs are also great for adding color to a shade garden at the start of the growing season.

Deciding What to Grow

While you can grow a garden that features only annuals or only perennials, there's no rule that says your garden can't include both—and more. In fact, the most appealing gardens are often creative blends of annuals and perennials, some with a sprinkling of roses, herbs, flowering shrubs, trees, bulbs, and even ornamental vegetables, as well. A mixed garden allows you to feature personal favorites and create a landscape that truly reflects your own individual taste.

FLOWER TYPES

Walk around a garden center or turn the pages of a seed catalog, and you'll see terms like annuals, perennials, biennials, and bulbs. But what do these terms mean, and how do you use them when planning a garden?

ANNUALS. These germinate, bloom, set seed, and die all in one season. You'll often see these plants described as either cool- or warm-weather annuals. *Cool-weather annuals*, including pansies and alyssum, grow best in spring and fall, when temperatures are cool. They also can be grown through winter in the South. *Warm-weather annuals*, including marigolds and zinnias, thrive in hot summer weather. Knowing whether a plant is a warm- or cool-weather annual is essential to scheduling it for top performance in your garden.

Another group of plants that are commonly treated as annuals are plants that are killed by frost at the end of the season. They include begonias and coleus. Also called *tender perennials*, these can be dug out in fall and overwintered indoors in areas of the country where they are not hardy—in other words, where they will not survive the typical winter weather. You can also take and root cuttings of many tender perennials.

PERENNIALS. Living two or more seasons, perennials need to be able to survive winter cold in a region. Peonies and daylilies are both long-lived perennials. Columbines are short-lived perennials that need to be replaced every couple years. See the USDA Hardiness Zone Map on page 109 to determine the average minimum winter low temperatures in your region, then use that information and the hardiness information from seed packets, plant tags, and/or seed catalogs to select perennials suitable for your garden.

BIENNIALS. These plants typically produce foliage the first year and flowers the second. Foxglove and hollyhock are both biennials. Like most biennials, they self-sow, producing new plants and flowers in subsequent years without any human help. You can sometimes grow biennials as annuals if you start them early, causing them to bloom the first season. Many will live a few years as short-lived perennials.

BULBS. These are plants with fleshy underground structures. They include true bulbs, such as daffodils, and plants with fleshy roots and stems, such as dahlias and tuberous begonias.

HERBS. This term is used to refer to any plant valued for its flavor, fragrance, or medicinal properties. Examples include basil, lavender, and rosemary.

TIPS FOR SELECTING ANNUALS AND PERENNIALS

• Choose annuals and perennials that will thrive in the amount of sun or shade your garden receives. No amount of wishing will make sun-loving plants thrive in shade, or shade plants in sun.

• For season-long color in a dull spot, use groups of annuals. If you want to dress up an all-green shrub border, for example, try adding a few groupings of annuals in front of the shrubs to inject an extra burst of color.

• Use annuals to give a perennial garden a much-needed midsummer boost. Add summer-blooming annuals in the spaces where spring bulbs, pansies, or early blooming perennials are dying back. You can pop them into any empty spots that appear.

• Pay special attention to foliage. This is especially important when selecting perennials, since they typically are only in bloom for a few weeks each year. Attractive foliage is the foundation of a well-designed garden.

CHOOSING THE RIGHT COLORS

Just as you'd think about color before painting a room, it's a good idea to consider flower color when you select annuals, perennials, and other plants for your garden. Here are some ideas to get you started:

Use Winning Color Combinations

Try one of these proven combinations with the help of a color wheel: *Monochromatic* designs combine all of the shades, tints, and tones of a single color. Use two colors opposite each other on the color wheel for a *complementary* color scheme. For an *analogous* design, pick three adjacent colors on the color wheel.

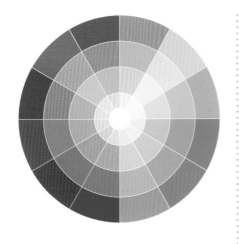

Use Color to Set the Mood

Think about the mood and atmosphere you'd like to create in each area of your garden. Create a nostalgic, romantic look by using pale pastels, or display a modern, upbeat style by mixing pure bright colors.

Consider Backdrops

Existing backgrounds, including fences, house walls, flowering shrubs, and other major landscape features, will affect your choice of flower colors. For example, if your house is painted white, you probably won't want to plant white flowers against it, because they'll be virtually invisible. If your garden is backed by dark woods or evergreens, flowers in dark shades of blue and purple will disappear against them, while white, yellow, silver-gray, and yellow-green blooms will stand out.

Try White and Silver

White flowers will heighten the contrast of any other colors you select. You can also use silver flowers or foliage to separate contrasting colors in a design.

Planning for Constant Bloom

While most annuals bloom all summer long, the majority of perennials have a limited season of bloom. So unless you opt for a garden built solely of annuals, you'll need to do a little planning to ensure that you will have new flowers coming into bloom week after week. That planning will pay ongoing dividends as you relish the anticipation and excitement of watching new flowers burst into bloom throughout the growing season. Use the following tips to guide your planning:

Build Up Your Perennial Repertoire

Perennials are the backbone of any garden, providing reliable beauty with minimal maintenance, and you'll want to have some blooming throughout your growing season. If you find yourself short of perennials that flower during certain times, check Perennials for Every Season on pages 35–39 for ideas.

Bank on Bulbs

Daffodils and other spring bulbs are great for adding spring color to the garden. Summer-blooming bulbs such as lilies, gladiolus, cannas, dahlias, and tuberous begonias add visual punch to early summer gardens.

Bridge Gaps with Annuals

Of course, combining annuals with your perennials is one way to ensure that you will have something pretty to look at all season long. But annuals can be especially useful in perking up your garden from mid-summer to early fall, when summertime heat and humidity reduce the number of perennials that are in bloom.

PERENNIALS FOR EVERY SEASON

The next several pages can help you select perennials that bloom in each part of the growing season.

EARLY SPRING

Hellebore (*Helleborus* species)

Epimedium (*Epimedium* species)

Lungwort (*Pulmonaria* species)

Columbine (*Aquilegia* species)

Candytuft (*Iberis sempervirens*)

Bleeding heart (*Dicentra* species)

False, or wild, indigo (*Baptisia australis*)

Poppy, Oriental (*Papaver orientale*)

Peony (*Paeonia* species)

Pink (*Dianthus* species)

Iris (*Iris* species)

Foxglove (*Digitalis purpurea*)

Plants with a * bloom until late summer or early fall.

Yarrow (*Achillea* species)

Beardtongue
(*Penstemon barbatus*)

Verbascum*
(*Verbascum* species)

Astilbe (*Astilbe* species)

Monarda, bee balm
(*Monarda didyma*)

Rudbeckia,
orange coneflower*
(*Rudbeckia* species)

Painted daisy (*Tanacetum coccineum*)

Cardinal flower (*Lobelia cardinalis*)

Daylily* (*Hemerocallis* species)

Coreopsis* (*Coreopsis* species)

Butterfly weed* (*Asclepias tuberosa*)

Blanket flower* (*Gaillardia × grandiflora*)

Shasta daisy (*Leucanthemum × superbum*)

Stokes' aster
(*Stokesia laevis*)

Hibiscus, rose mallow
(*Hibiscus moscheutos*)

Aster (*Aster* species)

Garden phlox
(*Phlox paniculata*)

Pincushion flower
(*Scabiosa caucasica*)

Goldenrod (*Solidago* species)

Salvia (*Salvia* species)

Lavender (*Lavandula angustifolia*)

Purple coneflower (*Echinacea purpurea*)

Toad lily (*Tricyrtis* species)

Chrysanthemum
(*Chrysanthemum* species)

Perovskia, Russian sage
(*Perovskia* species)

Japanese anemone
(*Anemone* species)

Eupatorium (*Eupatorium* species)

Aster (*Aster* species)

BEYOND FLOWERS

It's easy to get swept away by flowers, but you won't regret looking beyond blooms when selecting plants for your garden.

Consider Foliage

Perennials and annuals with outstanding foliage—leaves that look good all season or are colorfully patterned—are invaluable in the garden. Hostas are well known for bold leaves in shades from deep green to chartreuse, many with lighter markings. Silver-leaved dusty miller and colorful coleus are annuals grown for their foliage.

Try to include plants that sport leaves of different shapes and sizes and foliage of varying textures as well. Incorporating plants with assorted leaf styles adds contrast and interest to a garden, making it more dramatic and appealing. Achilleas and astilbes have feathery leaves, for example, while daylilies and ornamental grasses sport ribbonlike leaves. Attractive leaves also set off flowers more effectively.

Mix Heights and Forms

Pay attention to height, too, as you select plants for your garden. Include plants of differing height, so you have short selections for the front edges and taller ones to use in the middle of beds or at the back of borders.

Another variable to consider is shape, or form—in terms of both the plant as a whole and its flowers. Peonies and Shasta daisies, for example, have rounded forms. To make your garden more visually interesting, consider mixing such rounded plants with vase-shape plants such as daylilies and vertical plants like hollyhock and foxglove.

CREATING A DESIGN

The idea of selecting and arranging plants and colors in a garden probably sounds overwhelming, but don't get discouraged. Start by reviewing your plant list. For a small- to medium-size garden, you'll need six to eight perennials, plus some annuals and bulbs. There are two basic ways you can approach turning your list into a garden. One way involves planning the garden on paper; the other consists of shopping for the plants on your list and arranging them on the site. Either way, you'll avoid a common mistake most new gardeners make, because you'll already have a plant list before you purchase a single flower.

Before you start, review your list and confirm that each plant will thrive on your chosen site. Eliminate any plants that won't grow well there, and substitute more suitable ones.

INSTALLING YOUR GARDEN

Getting your garden off to a good start is an important and enjoyable process with a big payoff. The time and care you put in at this stage are well worth the effort. Your reward will be a gorgeous display of flowers.

Understanding Your Soil

Good soil is essential to a great garden. The loose, dark earth from which fabulous gardens spring doesn't usually just happen. It is created by gardeners. Whether you have dry, sandy soil that water runs straight through or heavy clay that stays wet for days before drying to the hardness of concrete, there's one thing you can do to improve it: Add organic matter. Digging plentiful doses of organic material—chopped leaves, ground-up twigs, rotted livestock manure, old lawn clippings—into the earth will improve and nourish any kind of soil, making it ideal for growing plants. *Compost*, made from decayed leaves, grass clippings, other yard waste, and even food scraps, is the single best choice for boosting soil. You can make your own or purchase it bagged at a garden center.

Identifying Your Soil Type

There are various ways to determine which kind of soil you're dealing with. For a quick test, simply squeeze some slightly moist soil in your hand. Clay soil forms a dense, compact lump that retains its shape. Sandy soil doesn't hold its shape at all. And loam soil forms a ball that falls apart if tapped with a finger. While adding compost and other organic matter will help all of these soil types, the following specific guidelines will help you fine-tune your garden's foundation:

CLAY SOIL. Never dig or plant in clay soil when it is wet. Be especially careful to avoid walking on clay soil, as well; it has a very dense structure, and walking on it compresses the small pores that hold the air and water that a plant's roots need.

SANDY SOIL. Keep sandy soil mulched at all times to hold it in place and help retain moisture. And get in the habit of adding compost every time you dig, since microbes in the soil use up organic matter quickly.

LOAM SOIL. This is the ideal garden soil, but don't rest on your laurels if you have it! Add compost and other organic matter regularly, and keep the soil mulched to protect it.

PREPARING THE GARDEN BED

Before planting that first flower in your new garden bed, you must prepare the garden bed. Begin by marking the boundaries: Use stakes and string to mark a square or rectangular bed and a garden hose to outline a bed with curved edges. Remove any grass or weeds from the area, then rototill or hand dig the soil, turning it over thoroughly. If the area is rocky, remove as many stones as possible as you till. Next, spread the necessary fertilizer, soil conditioners, and pH-adjusting products over the area. Till again. You should be able to till the soil more deeply the second time. Ideally, you want to loosen and improve the soil to a depth of more than 8 inches (bad soils may require 10–12 inches). Leave the bed unplanted for two weeks so the soil has time to settle before planting.

STARTING FROM SEED

While buying flats of annuals and pots of perennials is tempting because they create an instant display in the garden, starting your own plants from seed saves money and expands options. Many annuals and perennials, for example, are not commercially available as established plants, often because they simply don't transplant successfully and must be grown from seed. Starting from seed also makes sense if you have a large garden and need lots of plants to fill it. You can grow dozens of plants from seed for the cost of a single established perennial.

You can start seed indoors in market packs or individual pots, such as these, or you can sow seed directly into the garden bed.

How to Start Seed Indoors

You can start seed indoors by sowing them in a pot of soil on a windowsill. If you don't have a south-facing window that will receive adequate sun, consider investing in some seed-starting equipment and supplies.

LIGHT. The most essential ingredient is adequate light. Seedlings that do not receive enough light will stretch out toward the light source and become leggy. Invest in special grow lamps, or buy a simple fluorescent shop light and hang it with chain and "S" hooks so you can adjust the distance between it and the seedlings. (Maintain about three inches between the light and the plant tops at all times.) Give plants 16–18 hours of light daily.

HEAT. Bottom heat is another secret to successful seed starting. You can set trays of seedlings on a radiator or atop the refrigerator, or buy a commercial heat mat designed to heat soil.

SOIL. Although you can mix your own potting soil, it is simpler to purchase specially formulated seed-starting mix. Before filling potting containers, dump the mix in a large bucket or tub, add plenty of warm water, and stir. Wait until the mix has soaked up the water before filling the containers with it.

CONTAINERS. Seeds can be started in a variety of containers, provided the containers hold soil and allow easy passage of water through drainage holes. You can use milk cartons or plastic food containers with holes punched in the bottom, or you can purchase plastic or fiber pots or trays. You will also need shallow trays to catch water dripping from pots.

Move Seedlings into Pots

Seedlings in large containers or trays need to be transplanted to individual pots when the first true leaves appear. To do this, gently lift them out, separate them carefully, and replant them in individual pots. Always handle seedlings carefully. Hold them by a leaf, never by the stem, which is easily damaged. Place the seedling in the new container so the soil line will be at the same level on the stem as it was in the seed tray. Gently firm the soil around the roots. Water from the top with a weak fertilizer solution. Then place the plants back by the window or under grow lamps to continue growing.

How to Sow Seeds Outdoors

Many annuals can be successfully sown outdoors, directly into the garden. Just loosen the soil, work in organic matter, and rake it smooth to create a seed bed. Gently sprinkle the seeds over the site, then lightly rake the site again, and use a fine spray from a hose or watering can to briefly water the site. Water daily in dry weather.

TRANSPLANTING FROM POTS

Whether you're moving your homegrown seedlings or purchased plants into the garden, it pays to handle them with care. Use the following information to ease the transition.

Harden Off Sheltered Plants

Seedlings that you grew indoors or plants that were inside a greenhouse when you bought them will need to be hardened off. That's a gardener's term for gradually getting plants used to the conditions outdoors before you transplant them into your garden, so they don't suffer shock and/or wilt. To harden off your plants, first make sure they are well watered, then set them outside in a protected spot for an hour the first day. A site on the north side of a building or under an evergreen tree is ideal. After an hour, bring the plants indoors, then take them out the second day for a longer period of time. Gradually extend their daily outdoor time over the course of a week until they're ready to spend the night outdoors. Once you've hardened your plants this way, they're ready to be bedded down in your garden.

Tuck Them in Beds ASAP

Container-grown plants that are bound for the garden should be hardened and transplanted as soon as weather permits. Follow these steps for successful transplanting.

1. Submerge potted plants in water before transplanting. To avoid damage to the plant top and to help keep the root ball intact, spread your hand over the top of the pot with stems and leaves poking out between your fingers. Then turn the pot upside down and gently tap its rim against something solid to slide the plant from the container.

2. The roots need to spread out after planting, rather than continuing to grow in a tight mass. If they resist loosening with your fingers, cut up into the sides of the root ball in several places with a sharp knife or scissors, then shake the roots loose a bit more with your fingers before planting.

3. Firm soil around the plant stem and roots. Create a soil dam around the plant and fill it with water. The soaking water will help settle the soil and remove any remaining air pockets around the roots—air pockets can cause delicate feeder roots to dry out and die. Apply mulch around the crown and under trailing foliage.

DIVIDING PERENNIALS

Perennials—especially those that spread quickly—need to be dug up and divided every few years. Division helps keep perennials within bounds and gives you the chance to remove older, less vital portions of each clump. A natural by-product of this process is additional plants, which you can replant in your own garden or share with friends.

Separating Roots

Perennials can be divided by lifting an entire clump and cutting it apart or by taking pieces away from the clump's outer edges—separating the pieces from the main plant by cutting through the crown with a knife or sharp-bladed spade.

Try to keep as many of the roots intact as possible and to have some roots and some foliage in each division. Trim back excess top foliage to balance the loss of feeder roots that takes place when the plants are dug up and torn apart. Avoid the impulse to get as many separate clumps as possible: Larger clumps will thrive, while small divisions are likely to struggle and grow very slowly.

Always plant the new divisions at the same depth they were growing before you dug up the original clump. Firm the soil around each new plant, and water well to help settle the soil closely around the roots. Be sure to deeply water new divisions as needed during their first weeks in the garden.

Timing

Except in the South, the best time to divide most perennials is early spring. But you should wait to divide early-spring bloomers until right after they're done flowering. And there are a few plants—peonies, irises, and Oriental poppies—that, despite being summer bloomers, do better if they're divided after they've finished flowering and begun to change color. In the South, fall is a better time to divide all perennials except Oriental poppies.

Container Gardening

Growing flowers in containers is a fun, creative, and easy way to garden, whether you want to add single spots of color to a patio or plant an entire grouping of containers. You can even garden in containers on a rooftop, a high-rise balcony, a raised deck, a fire escape, or a yard covered with concrete. Use the following suggestions to select and plant a successful container garden.

Container plants can be used to brighten walkways, steps, and other areas where there is little or no soil.

Choose Your Containers

All that's essential is that the container be capable of holding soil and allowing excess water to drain away. Large containers are generally better than small ones because the soil in them dries out more slowly and plants' roots don't overheat as quickly. Choose from terra cotta, ceramic, plastic, lightweight resin, and wood containers. And don't forget to consider hanging baskets or window boxes.

Care for Containers Regularly

A container garden needs daily attention. Check soil moisture every evening. When the weather is dry and windy, check it morning and evening. To determine if plants need watering, rub a pinch of soil between your thumb and finger. If the soil feels at all dry to the touch, water. On the other hand, the soil should not be constantly soaking wet, because the plants will drown. When watering, be sure water reaches all of the soil in the container: Fill the planter to the rim with water several times, allowing it to soak in completely. If no water comes out of the drainage holes, fill again. Repeat this process until water starts to drip from the bottom of the container. Also pinch and deadhead potted plants regularly to keep them blooming and looking their best. Fertilize every ten days with liquid fertilizer; dilute it to the recommended strength for containers, as directed on the label.

Fill Containers Generously

Use commercial or homemade potting mix to fill them. Plant a single annual per pot, or create a more lavish display by filling each container with several annuals. When combining plants in a container, include different flower colors and foliage textures to add interest. Ideally, use one eye-catching plant as a focal point, and blend others in around it.

ANNUALS FOR CONTAINERS

A great many annuals can thrive in a container garden. These are some of the best:

Begonias

Marigolds

Coleus

Geraniums

Nasturtiums

Petunias

Impatiens

Pansies

PERENNIALS FOR CONTAINERS

Perennials—both hardy and tender—make handsome container plants. Keeping tender plants in pots makes it especially easy to move them indoors over the winter. Try some of these perennial favorites:

Scabiosa

Ferns

Rudbeckias

Lavender

Shasta daisies

Salvias

Daylilies

Sedums

Gaillardias

Hostas

Chrysanthemums

Chapter 4

PLANT PROFILES

In this chapter, you will find information on a wide variety of annuals, perennials, and other flowering plants. Perusing these pages is sure to inspire new plantings for your flower garden or different blooms to include in flower arrangements. You'll find flowers listed alphabetically by their most popular common name. Other common names are then sometimes listed, and each plant's botanical name and vital information follows. Plant descriptions and color photographs will help you discern what they can contribute to your flower garden. The entries also include how to grow each plant, uses, related species and varieties, and, if applicable, compatible USDA hardiness zones (see page 109 for USDA Plant Hardiness Zone Map).

Description: Fast-growing amaranths tolerate poor soil, heat, and drought. The genus contains several notable ornamental plants. *A. tricolor*, commonly called Joseph's coat, is 3 to 5 feet tall and produces foliage in yellow, red, orange, and green. *A. caudatus* is often called tassel flower for its cascading ropelike blooms.

How to grow: Give amaranths full sun and well-drained soil. Wet soil and poor drainage cause root rot and death. Tall varieties may require staking.

Propagation: Start seeds indoors, or sow directly outdoors, but don't sow or move plants outdoors until all chance of frost has passed. Germination takes 7 days at 70° to 75°F.

Uses: Use amaranths in beds and borders. With varieties ranging from 20 inches to 5 feet or greater, these showy gems work well in the back of the border, alone in a mass planting or alongside other tall annuals like sunflowers, cleome, and zinnias. Also use *A. caudatus* in containers and for cutting.

Related species and varieties: *A. tricolor* 'Flaming Fountains' has long, willowy, crimson leaves. *A. caudatus* 'Love-Lies-Bleeding' bears drooping spikes of blood-red flowers. *A. hypochondriacus*, commonly called prince's feather, has flowers held in upright panicles in shades of purple, red, gold, and green.

Left: Commonly known as 'Love-Lies-Bleeding,' *Amaranthus caudatus* can grow 3 to 5 feet high with long panicles of dangling flowers.

AMARANTH
(Amaranthus species)
Type: Annual

Amaranthus tricolor, sometimes called Joseph's coat or summer poinsettia, is a popular species that produces leaves in tropical colors.

Hardiness: Zones 3 to 8

Description: Astilbes are lovely plants both for their handsome, fernlike foliage and their long panicles (or spikes) of flowers that resemble feathery plumes. Bloom time varies, with selections flowering anytime from late spring to late summer. Each plant blooms for about 3 weeks, but foliage looks great for the duration of the growing season.

ASTILBE, GARDEN SPIREA
(*Astilbe* species)
Type: Perennial

How to grow: Astilbes can be grown in full sun in cool northern regions but are best with partial shade, especially in the southern United States. Soil should be rich, moist, and have plenty of organic matter mixed in. Divide the clumps every third or fourth year.

Propagation: Divide clumps in early spring or sow seeds outdoors in pots.

Uses: Use astilbes in beds and borders. They mix well with hostas and ferns. Heights vary from 12 to 40 inches. Colors include white, pink, red, rose, cranberry, and lavender. The white forms are especially effective against a shrub border or a line of bushes. They also make an effective ground cover. Astilbes can be used as cut flowers in the summer and dried for winter floral arrangements.

Related varieties: 'Bridal Veil' bears white flowers on 2-foot stems; 'Fanal' blooms early with deep red flowers. 'Rheinland' is another early bloomer; it's a hardy plant with rich pink flowers. 'Purple Candle' has deep purple, chenille-like plumes. 'Vision in Red' is a compact plant with dark purplish red flowers.

Astilbes can add interesting color and texture to bouquets like the one shown here.

BABY'S BREATH
(Gypsophila paniculata)
Type: Perennial

Baby's breath plants belong to the *Caryophyllaceae* family, which includes other flowers like the dianthus and carnation.

Hardiness: Zones 4 to 9

Description: Their light, airy texture and petite white or pink flowers make baby's breath a wonderful addition to the garden. They feature small, blue-green leaves and a profusion of many-branched white-flowering panicles. Plants bloom in June and July.

How to grow: Baby's breath require full sun and a deep, well-drained lime-rich garden soil. Even though the plants have taproots, they still require liberal amounts of water. Tall plants will probably require staking. They will rebloom if spent flowers are removed.

Propagation: By seed

Uses: Baby's breath are effective in borders or cottage gardens. They are especially lovely when tumbling over rock walls or falling out of a raised bed. Baby's breath also make a superb cut flower.

Related species and varieties: The most popular variety is 'Bristol Fairy,' with white double flowers, which grows to a height of 4 feet. Related species include *Gypsophila repens*, a pink or white creeping baby's breath that grows 3 to 6 inches high. *Gypsophila elegans* is considered an annual and performs well in wildflower meadows.

Almost everyone has seen a bouquet or boutonniere that contained a few sprays of baby's breath.

Description: Bachelor's buttons grow 1 to 3 feet tall with innumerable round flowers held above the rather sparse, long and narrow gray-green leaves. The habit of growth is relatively loose.

How to grow: Full sun in average soil is good. For earliest bloom, sow seeds outdoors in the fall so they will start to grow before the first frost and bloom the next spring. Otherwise, sow seeds outdoors as early in the spring as the soil can be worked. Thin to 8 to 12 inches apart.

Propagation: To grow seedlings indoors, germinate at 65°F four weeks before planting out. Germination time is 7 to 14 days.

Uses: Bachelor's buttons lend themselves to informal planting, particularly with other annuals and perennials in beds and borders. The flowers dry well, but stems are weak and must be wired for arrangements.

Related varieties: 'Blue Boy' grows to 2½ feet. 'Polka Dot Mixed' and 'Frosty Mixed' have white or pastel contrasts at petal tips.

BACHELOR'S BUTTON, CORNFLOWER

(Centaurea cyanus)

Type: Annual

Bachelor's button is a common boutonniere flower and is reputedly where this favorite got its name.

Hardiness: Zone 4

Description: Balloon flowers are clump-forming perennials with alternate leaves of light green on stems that usually grow between 1½ and 3 feet tall. They bear 2- to 3-inch balloon-shaped buds that open to bell-shaped flowers with five points.

How to grow: Balloon flowers like moist, well-drained soil in full sun or partial shade. They prefer places with cool summers. Plan the plant's position carefully as it is not until late spring that the first signs of life appear.

Propagation: By division in mid-spring or by seed

Uses: Balloon flowers bloom during most of the summer and are attractive in borders. Smaller types grow best along garden edges. They are especially effective when used in conjunction with white pansies, the white obedient plant, or bright yellow yarrow.

BALLOON FLOWER

(Platycodon grandifloras)

Type: Perennial

A one-species genus, balloon flowers are so named because the unopened flowers look like small hot-air balloons.

BASKET-OF-GOLD, GOLDENTUFT
(Aurinia saxatilis)

Type: Perennial

Hardiness: Zones 3 and 4

Description: Attractive, low gray foliage growing in dense mats gives support to clusters of golden-yellow, four-petaled flowers floating 6 to 12 inches above the plants.

How to grow: *Aurinias* need only well-drained, average soil in full sun. Plants will easily rot in damp locations and resent high humidity. They can be sheared after blooming.

Propagation: By cuttings or by seed

Uses: *Aurinias* are quite happy growing in the spaces between stone walks, carpeting a rock garden, or growing in pockets in stone walls where their flowers become tumbling falls of gold.

Once included in the *Alyssum* genus, these charming flowers now belong to the mustard family.

BEARD-TONGUE, PENSTEMON
(Penstemon barbatus)

Type: Perennial

Hardiness: Zones 4 to 8

Description: Basal foliage is evergreen in warmer climates. The leaves are sometimes whorled. Flowers are tubular in airy, terminal clusters atop strong stems, blooming from spring into summer.

How to grow: Penstemons come from areas with rough growing conditions and should never be planted in soil that stays wet or damp. A thin, rocky soil in full sun is best.

Propagation: By division in spring or by seed

Uses: Penstemons are exceedingly attractive in the garden and have a long season of bloom. Plants look best set out in groups so that a mass of flowers is in view. Some gardeners succumb to their beauty and are inspired to create entire specialty gardens out of this genus. They are excellent as cut flowers.

Related varieties: Perhaps the most well-known variety is 'Husker Red,' which features reddish-purple foliage and white flowers. 'Elfin Pink' has clear pink flowers on 1-foot-high branches, making it perfect for the front of the border.

Penstemon plants are herbaceous perennials. Flower colors include pink, red, white, purple, and rarely yellow.

Hardiness: Zones 3 to 7

Description: Sturdy, square stems growing to 4 feet tall have simple leaves. They are topped by crowns studded with lipped, usually bright red, pink, purple, or white flowers blooming from summer into fall.

How to grow: Full sun and slightly moist soil are best for *monardas*; they become somewhat floppy when grown in the shade. To reduce mildew problems, plant where air circulation is good. These plants are vigorous spreaders, so excess plants should be removed from time to time.

Propagation: By seed or by division in early spring

Uses: Useful for the wild garden in moist soil or by the waterside, they are also beautiful in beds or borders because of their long season of bright bloom. The flowers are beloved by hummingbirds and butterflies.

Related species and varieties: 'Jacob Cline' is mildew resistant. 'Petite Delight' is 12 to 15 inches tall and bears pink flowers. The flowers of *Monarda fistulosa*, or wild bergamot, are light lavender or whitish pink.

BEE BALM, BERGAMOT, OSWEGO TEA

(Monarda didyma)

Type: Perennial

Monarda didyma is native to eastern North America where it is typically found in bottomlands, thickets, moist woodlands, and along streambanks.

Bee balm attracts bees, hummingbirds, and butterflies, particularly when plants are massed.

BEGONIA
(*Begonia* species)

Type: Annual, tender perennial, bulb

Wax begonia (*Begonia semperflorens*) is a popular garden annual. The compact, bushy, mounded, fibrous-rooted plant features fleshy stems, waxy dark green to bronze leaves, and loose clusters of flowers in shades of white, pink, or red, plus bi-color varieties.

Hardiness: Zones 8 to 10

Description: Handsome leaves and showy flowers make begonias a garden favorite. Most bear blooms in white or shades of pink, rose, or red. About 1,300 species of annuals, perennials, shrubs, and climbers make up the *Begonia* genus. Most have fleshy stems. Some produce underground tubers or rhizomes. Popular wax begonias (*Begonia semperflorens*) are mounding 8- to 10-inch-high plants. Other garden types are taller, growing to about 15 inches.

How to grow: Most begonias do well in partial shade to shade and rich, moist, well-drained soil. Wax begonias also grow in full sun, except in hot climates.

Propagation: Start wax begonias from seed or buy plants. Sow the dustlike seeds in winter, following seed packet directions carefully. Germination temperature is 70° to 85°F and requires 14 to 21 days. Cuttings also root readily. A good way to start plants is on a sunny windowsill during winter. Start tuberous begonias indoors in late winter about 2½ to 3 months before planting out in the garden. Transplant bulbs only after all threat of frost has passed.

Uses: Wax begonias lend themselves to large, formal plantings because of their uniform size and shapeliness. They're also suitable in front of summer annual borders and combine well with other cool-colored flowers in mixed plantings and containers. Use tuberous begonias in containers, window boxes, hanging baskets, and in garden borders.

Related species and varieties: Many colors and forms of wax begonia are available. The most popular, dark-leaved kinds are the Cocktail series: 'Brandy,' 'Vodka,' 'Whiskey,' and 'Gin.' Good green-leaved varieties are found in the Olympia and Prelude series. 'Avalanche' begonias in pink or white are rangier, suited for containers and hanging baskets, where their arching growth habit is handsome.

Tuberous begonias belong to the Tuberosa group, a large and diverse group of tender, summer-flowering plants featuring brightly colored waxy-petaled flowers in shades of white, yellow, apricot, pink, rose, and red. Plants typically grow 12 to 18 inches tall.

BELLFLOWER

(*Campanula* species)
Type: Perennial

The botanical name is from the Latin word for "bell" and refers to the shape of the flowers.

Hardiness: Zone 4

Description: Bellflowers are usually various shades of blue or white and bloom from late spring into early summer.

How to grow: Bellflowers need a good, moist, but well-drained soil with plenty of organic matter mixed in. In the North, plants will tolerate full sun as long as the soil is not dry, but elsewhere a spot in semi-shade is preferred.

Propagation: By division, cuttings, or seed

Uses: Plants are beautiful in the border, useful in the rock garden, and fine for the shade or wild garden.

Related species: *C. carpatica* blooms at a height of 10 inches with solitary blue flowers. It is effective as an edging, or tumbling over a small rock cliff. *C. poscharskyana*, or Serbian bellflower, is a ground creeper with star-shaped, 1-inch blossoms of lavender-blue, perfect for the partially shaded, dry rock garden or a hanging basket. *C. rotundifolia*, also known as harebell, is very cold tolerant and looks best when grown in mountain or northern regions. Canterbury bells (*C. medium*) is a popular 1- to 3-foot-tall biennial.

Campanula rotundifolia is known as harebell, or bluebells of Scotland.

Serbian bellflower (*Campanula poscharskyana*)

Campanula carpatica

Bells of Ireland
(Moluccella laevis)
Type: Annual

Description: Bells of Ireland produce dramatic 3-foot-tall spires of large, showy green bells (or calyxes), each hiding tiny white or pinkish true flowers inside. The flowers are fragrant.

How to grow: Give plants full sun or partial shade and average, well-drained soil. Thin seedlings to space plants 12 inches apart. To prevent their toppling, plant them in areas protected from high wind or tie them to a bamboo stake.

Propagation: In zones 3 to 6, sow seeds outdoors 2 to 3 weeks before the last spring frost date. From zone 7 south, sow in fall for spring germination. Or sow indoors in individual pots 8 to 10 weeks before the last spring frost, and store pots for 2 weeks in the refrigerator before germinating them at 55°F, which takes 1 to 4 weeks.

Uses: Plant this stately annual at the rear of garden borders for a vertical thrust. Especially revered by flower arrangers, the light green flowers hold their color for a long time in arrangements.

Hardiness: Zones 4 and 5

Description: *Epimediums* have sturdy, heart-shaped leaves with a toothed edge on wiry stems that closely resemble a jester's hat or, in some species, a bishop's miter or biretta. They bloom in April and May.

Distinctive foliage and delicate flowers make *epimediums* a wonderful addition to any garden. They grow naturally in bright woodlands with light shade.

How to grow:
Epimediums like good, well-drained, somewhat moist garden soil in open shade, although they will tolerate some sun. They grow well under tree canopies and easily coexist with tree roots. *Epimediums* are slow to establish but do spread gradually. Cut old foliage off in early spring before the new growth begins.

Bishop's Hat, Barrenwort
(Epimedium species)
Type: Perennial

Propagation: By division in late spring after flowering is finished or by seed

Uses: Classified by most nurseries as a ground cover, *epimediums* are also excellent for the edge of a border. Some of the species are evergreen where the climate allows. They mix well with hostas and are a good choice to plant under Japanese maples or large shade trees.

Hardiness: Zones 3 to 7

Description: *Rudbeckias* bear daisylike flowers with dark centers and gold, yellow, orange, rust, or maroon petals, many with bands of contrasting colors. Varieties of black-eyed Susan grow from 1 to 3 feet tall.

How to grow: Bright sun is the main requirement. It will tolerate poor soil and draught. Transplant into the garden after the last spring frost date. Space plants 10 to 15 inches apart. Cutting the flowers encourages increased blooming.

Propagation: By seed. Treated as biennials or perennials, the seeds can be sown in the garden the preceding summer or fall. For bloom the same season, start seeds indoors 8 to 10 weeks prior to transplanting. Seeds germinate in 5 to 10 days at 70° to 75°F.

Uses: They'll do well in large containers and are good cut flowers.

Although a short-lived perennial, the black-eyed Susan (*R. hirta*) blooms the first year from seed and is often grown as an annual.

BLACK-EYED SUSAN, GLORIOSA DAISY
(*Rudbeckia hirta*)
Type: Annual, perennial

Related species and varieties: 'Cherokee Sunset,' an All-America Selections winner, is a mix of yellow, orange, and red doubles. Biennial 'Indian Summer' bears 6- to 9-inch-wide golden flowers. Perennial 'Goldsturm' (*R. fulgida var. sullivantii*) bears 3- to 4-inch-wide flowers.

Hardiness: Grown as an annual in zones 3 to 9; grown as a perennial in zones 10 and 11

Description: A native of tropical East Africa, black-eyed Susan vine can grow 6 to 8 feet tall in a season and has rough, hairy leaves. The blooms have five distinct petals. Flower color can be white, yellow, orange, or cream. Most have dark centers.

Thunbergia alata is a tender perennial climbing vine that is normally grown as an annual.

BLACK-EYED SUSAN VINE, CLOCK VINE
(*Thunbergia alata*)
Type: Vine

How to grow: Generally, it grows best in full sun. It needs average, well-drained soil. Plant seedlings 3 inches away from supports. Space plants 5 to 8 inches apart. Pinch the tips to encourage branching. Black-eyed Susan vines will need a trellis to climb large posts or solid fencing.

Propagation: By seed or by cuttings. Sow seeds outdoors after the last frost or start seedlings indoors 6 to 8 weeks before outdoor planting. Seeds germinate in 10 to 15 days at 70° to 75°F. Cuttings root easily in a commercial soil mix.

Uses: *Thunbergias* can be used to cover posts, porches, arbors, pergolas, or fences. They also make good container plants. Plants in containers will also bloom over winter in sunny windows.

BLAZINGSTAR, GAYFEATHER
(*Liatris* species)
Type: Perennial

Hardiness: Zones 3 to 9

Description: Simple, linear leaves on usually stout stems grow in clumps from thick rootstocks. Flower heads are set along tall spikes and bear fluffy disk flowers resembling feathery staffs.

How to grow: Blazingstars need good, well-drained soil in full sun to succeed. Wet, winter soil will usually kill the plants. The taller varieties sometimes require staking. They are especially valuable as cut flowers.

Propagation: By division of older plants in spring or by seed

Uses: Clumps of blazingstars are perfect for meadow plantings and cottage gardens, where they will attract butterflies. They're also popular in summer bouquets and vase arrangements.

Related species and varieties: Three commonly available *Liatris* species include *spicata*, *aspera*, and *pycostachya* types.

Liatris pycostachya, commonly called prairie blazingstar, is native to Missouri.

Hardiness: Zones 3 to 9

Description: Bleeding heart has clusters of rose, pink, or white flowers on arching sprays of fernlike foliage. It grows 24 to 30 inches tall with a spread of 18 to 30 inches. It is one of the earliest perennials to flower in the shaded garden.

BLEEDING HEART
(*Lamprocapnos spectabilis*)
Type: Perennial

How to grow: Bleeding hearts need full or partial shade with an evenly moist, slightly acidic soil. Plenty of compost should be added when planting; mulch around bleeding heart with pine needles or pine bark.

Propagation: By division in early spring or by seed; roots are fleshy and sold by the number of eyes present on plant starts.

These heart-shaped pendant flowers with spurs at the base have attractive foliage until midsummer.

Uses: This plant is a lovely sight when planted in a shady bed or woodland border.

Description: Blue marguerite is erect in growth, from 1 to 2 feet tall. It has glossy, deep green leaves with flowers on relatively short stems in sky-blue to darker shades, centered with a yellow eye.

How to grow: Blue marguerite thrives in moist but well-drained soil, in full sun to partial shade. Truly hot weather causes their decline, making them best as a summer plant for maritime or mountain climates. Plant outside after all danger of frost has passed, spacing them 9 to 12 inches apart.

Propagation: Trailing forms are available only through cuttings; seed-grown plants are mostly upright. Sow seeds 6 to 8 weeks prior to planting out. Germination takes up to 30 days at 70°F.

Uses: Plant in garden beds and borders, or use in containers.

Related species: *Felicia bergeriana*, the 'kingfisher daisy,' grows to a height of about 8 inches—smaller than *F. amelloides*. It has longer and more narrow leaves and bright blue flowers with yellow centers.

BLUE MARGUERITE
(Felicia amelloides)
Type: Annual

BLUESTAR, BLUE-DOGBANE, BLUE-STAR-OF-TEXAS
(Amsonia tabernaemontana)
Type: Perennial

Bluestars are native wildflowers found in wooded areas and on river banks from New Jersey to Tennessee to Texas.

Hardiness: Zones 3 to 9

Description: Blooming in May and June, bluestars have five petals and are a lovely pale blue color. After flowering has terminated, the upright stems with narrow leaves are still attractive. In the fall, the foliage turns a beautiful butterscotch-yellow.

How to grow: Plants should be established in any reasonably fertile garden soil. They grow between 2 and 3 feet tall and are somewhat tolerant of dry soil. Blossoms are better when given full sun, but bluestars will tolerate just a bit of shade. They will self-sow, with seedlings becoming bushy clumps in a few years.

Propagation: By division in the early spring

Uses: Bluestars belong in any wild garden and in beds or borders. They are especially attractive mixed with wild or garden columbines (*Aquilegia* species) and planted in the vicinity of tree peonies.

Boltonias are native American wildflowers found in poor or damp soil as far north as Manitoba, Canada, south to Florida, and west to Texas.

BOLTONIA
(Boltonia asteroides)
Type: Perennial

Hardiness: Zone 4

Description: Plants resemble asters with sturdy stems, narrow leaves, and dozens of white flowers in clusters. Blooming from late summer into fall, a well-situated boltonia will be covered with bloom.

How to grow: Boltonias prefer well-drained, moist, organic soil and full sun. It will tolerate periods of drought and can be grown in light shade if you are willing to stake it. Divide every four to five years to control spread.

Propagation: By division in spring or fall

Uses: Since boltonias grow 5 to 8 feet high, they are best at the rear of the garden. A line of these plants will become a flowering hedge of great charm. They can be used with ornamental grasses or mixed with fall asters.

Hardiness: Zones 3b to 8b

Description: Most spireas are spring-bloomers with numerous tiny white or pink flowers. Bridal-wreath grows 6 to 8 feet in height, spreading 10 to 12 feet in diameter. It has a distinctly fountain-like growth habit, with a round top and arching branches recurving to the ground, covered with tufts of little white flowers all the way. Its leaves are greenish-blue, turning plum-colored in the fall.

How to grow: Although the shrub will grow well in medium shade, full sun produces more flowers. Bridal-wreath adapts well to most soils. To keep the shrub in top shape, prune back one-third of the old flowering wood annually after it finishes blooming.

Uses: An excellent accent plant, bridal-wreath is also good for informal hedges or screens and is well suited to mixed shrub borders.

Related species: Garland spirea (*Spiraea x arguta*) is similar to bridal-wreath but has less pendulous branches and a better covering of flowers in spring. The bumald spireas (*Spiraea x bumalda*) are summer-flowering spireas with pink to whitish flowers.

BRIDAL-WREATH
(Spiraea x vanhouttei)
Type: Shrub

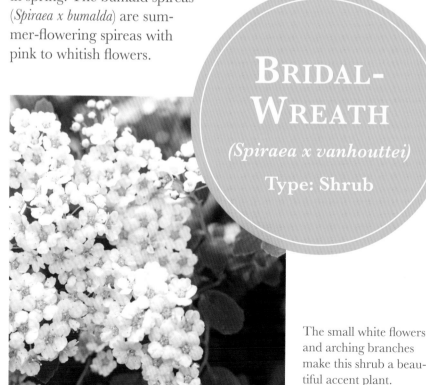

The small white flowers and arching branches make this shrub a beautiful accent plant.

BUTTERFLY WEED, MILKWEED

(Asclepias tuberosa)

Type: Perennial

Hardiness: Zone 4

Description: Blooming from late spring into summer, the individual orange-shaded flowers are striking in their beauty. The plants bear thin leaves and are most attractive when in flower.

How to grow: Butterfly weed tolerates a wide variety of soil types, but performs best in an average garden setting with full sun and good drainage. Once a butterfly weed develops a good root system, it becomes a long-lived, drought-resistant plant.

Propagation: By seed or by division in early spring

All members of the milkweed family are host plants for monarch butterflies and their young.

Uses: Butterfly weed does well in meadows and in wild gardens. The flowers can be cut for fresh bouquets. The seed pods are also used in dried arrangements.

Related species: The swamp milkweed, *Asclepias incarnata*, has pinkish flowers on 2- to 4-foot stems and grows well in wet situations.

CALADIUM

(Caladium hortulanum)

Type: Annual

Description: Large, spear- or arrowhead-shaped leaves on long stems rise directly from the tuber buried in the ground below. Depending on conditions, each leaf can grow up to 12 inches in length.

How to grow: Plant tubers directly in the ground after the soil has warmed, or start them early indoors in pots and plant them outside when the weather is warm. Caladiums thrive in high temperature and humidity. Outdoors, grow caladiums in moist, rich soil, and protect them from intense sun. In the fall, dig tubers before frost, allowing them to gradually dry off. Store in a frost-free location.

Propagation: Multiply plants by cutting tubers in pieces, similar to potatoes, being sure each piece retains growing "eyes."

Uses: Caladiums are unsurpassed for foliage color in beds, borders, or window boxes. Grow in moist areas to reduce water needs.

Related varieties: 'Candidum' is white with green leaves and ribs; 'Pink Beauty' is pink with a green background; and 'Frieda Hemple' is solid red with a green border.

Caladiums are grown entirely for their brightly colored and wildly patterned foliage.

CALLA LILY
(*Zantedeschia aethiopica*)
Type: Bulb

Zantedeschia aethiopica features a yellow spadix (long middle spike) surrounded by a white spathe (sheath) enclosing it.

Description: Though commonly called calla lilies, *Zantedeschia aethiopica* are not true lilies but rather members of the arum family. These natives of South Africa are perennials in zones 8 to 10, but are grown as annuals in other parts of the country since they are not tolerant of frost. Gardeners throughout the country can enjoy their lush, green leaves and bright flowers in summer by planting the tuber each spring.

How to grow: Start rhizomes indoors 8 weeks prior to warm weather. Plant the large tubers in a soil mix high in peat or other organic matter and grow at 70°F. Keep uniformly moist and fertilize weekly with a water-soluble fertilizer. Plant outside in a rich soil high in organic matter that retains moisture. Incorporate a slow-release fertilizer before planting. Grow in full sun for maximum growth. In the fall, lift before frost, drying off foliage and rhizomes. Store in a frost-free place until spring.

Propagation: Buy rhizomes at garden centers in the spring. Check to make sure they are firm and moist.

Uses: Plant callas anywhere you want to achieve a tropical look. They also make dramatic container plants and superb cut flowers.

Related species: *Z. rehmanni* is the pink calla, although it shows much variation in spathe color from wine-red to nearly white. It is smaller, growing 12 to 18 inches. *Z. elliotiana* is a species with white, spotted foliage, and a golden-yellow spathe.

Glistening, white calla lilies grow to 2 feet above the arrowhead-shaped leaves that arise from the rhizome planted below ground.

Zantedeschias are now available in a wide range of colors.

Hardiness: Zones 3 and 4

Description: Candytuft is a many-branched, small, evergreen shrub with smooth, oblong leaves about 1 ½ inches long. In the spring, it bears flat-topped clusters of white flowers, sometimes flushed with pink. Height can reach 10 inches, spreading to about 20 inches.

How to grow: Candytuft needs a good, well-drained garden soil in a sunny spot. They are usually evergreen, but in most areas of zone 4, winter results in severe damage to the leaves. Mulching is necessary if snow is lacking. Dead branches need to be cut off for growth to begin again. Pruning back after spring flowering is recommended.

Propagation: By seed or by division

Uses: Candytuft is great for a rock garden where it can tumble around and over rocks. It is also excellent as edging in a border and is well suited to growing in pots.

Related varieties: The 'Alexander's White' cultivar grows 10 to 12 inches tall and flowers heavily. 'Autumn Snow' stays about 10 inches high and blooms both in spring and fall. 'Little Gem' is a dwarf at a height of 6 inches.

CANDYTUFT
(Iberis sempervirens)
Type: Perennial

Many species of candytuft originally came from Iberia, the ancient name of Spain—hence the genus of *Iberis*. They bloom in spring.

CANNA
(Canna species)
Type: Bulb

Description: Cannas grow from fleshy roots with erect stalks from which broad, long leaves emerge. Flower stalks rising in the center bear large flowers. Foliage may be green, bronze, or purplish in hue.

How to grow: Cannas need full sun and grow best in a deep, rich, moist, but well-drained soil. Plant roots directly into the ground after soil is warm and all danger of frost has passed. Use pieces of rootstock with 2 or 3 large eyes and plant two inches deep. Space about 1 ½ to 2 feet apart.

Propagation: Few varieties are available by seed. Cut roots into pieces, each with 2 to 3 eyes, in the spring just prior to planting.

Uses: Use cannas in the center of island beds, at the sides or back of brightly colored borders, or near pools and ponds.

Related varieties: Tall varieties include: 'Yellow King Humbert,' yellow with scarlet flecks; 'The President,' bright crimson; and 'City of Portland,' a deep pink. Dwarf kinds growing to 2 ½ feet tall are available in several colors.

Description: Also called annual asters, popular China asters produce single, semi-double, and double flowers on 1- to 2½-foot-tall plants. Flowers come in shades of white, purple, pink, yellow, blue, or red. Bloom times differ too, with early summer, midsummer, and late summer varieties. For a continuous show, you'll need to pick different varieties and/or stagger sowing dates.

How to grow: China asters need full sun, rich soil, and ample water. Two disease problems have plagued them in the past: aster yellows, carried by leafhoppers, and fusarium wilt, a soil-borne disease. Select disease-resistant cultivars when buying seeds or plants. Sow seeds indoors or sow outdoors after the last spring frost date. Germination takes 10 to 20 days at 70°F. Plants will bloom only 3 to 4 weeks, so sow new crops every 10 days.

Propagation: By seed

Uses: Use China asters in beds, borders, cottage gardens, cutting gardens, or in pots and containers.

Related species and varieties: 'Pinocchio' is a dwarf strain of mixed colors with a garden mum flower form and garden habit. 'Perfection Mixed' plants grow to 2 feet with 4-inch fully double flowers. Super Giants Mixture grows to 2½ feet with 5-inch double spidery flowers. The Matsumo series is wilt-resistant. 'Violet Striped' is the best of the series.

CHINA ASTER

(Callistephus chinensis)

Type: Annual

From one highly variable species has come a whole range of China asters—singles, semi-doubles, and doubles, as well as tall, medium, and dwarf—all in a wide range of colors.

To condition asters, remove the lower leaves, scrape the stems, break or cut off the ends, and place the stems in water. They will last one to two weeks if you replace the water, and regularly remove the dead flowers.

Hardiness: Zones 4 to 6

Description: Popular chrysanthemums, or "mums," have strong stems and showy flowers. Leaves are usually divided and often aromatic.

How to grow: Chrysanthemums need full sun and good, well-drained, evenly moist soil. Garden mums should be fertilized two or three times during the growing season. They benefit from frequent pinching, which promotes bushy growth and more flowers. Divide plants in the spring every two years to maintain strong growth and good flowering.

Propagation: By stem cuttings, by division, or by seed

Uses: Chrysanthemums are perennial in some gardens but are usually best treated as annuals. In the fall, potted mums can be purchased from garden centers and transplanted around the garden where they will continue to bloom until severe frost cuts them down. Garden mums can be used in masses in front of ornamental grasses or to fill in areas where annuals have peaked and need to be replaced. They also do well in containers.

Related species: *C. paludosum* grows about 10 inches in height and has a mounding, trailing habit that spreads to 15 inches. The single, small, white flowers are borne profusely all over the plant. *C. multicaule* is slightly more vigorous, growing to 12 inches with a 20-inch spread. Flowers are single yellow daisies and are visible from a distance. Both will bloom all summer, but if bloom diminishes, shear back by half to encourage new growth and flowering.

Left: Chrysanthemums are members of the daisy clan, numbering more than 200 species of ornamental plants.

CHRYSANTHEMUM

(Chrysanthemum species*)*

Type: Annual, perennial

Garden mums (*Chrysanthemum x morifolium*) come in a number of flower styles and colors.

Hardiness: Zones 4a to 6b

Description: The plant's 4- to 7-inch, deep violet flowers with flattened sepals are well known by gardeners. Jackman's clematis climbs by wrapping its leaf petioles around narrow objects and can reach 12 feet in height. Its leaves are dark green and pinnate. The fuzzy seed heads are another point of attraction.

How to grow: Plant so that the roots are in a cool, shady spot but the upper growth is in full sun (for example, at the base of a shrub). The soil should be light, organic, and well-drained, but not constantly wet. Use an abundant cover of mulch. Clematis grows well in alkaline soil but does not require it. In early spring, prune to the ground those plants that, like Jackman's clematis, start anew from their base in the spring. Those that bloom on old wood (usually early spring-bloomers) should only be pruned lightly. In cold climates, mound plentiful soil at the base of the plant for the winter.

Uses: Jackman's clematis is spectacular for use on rock walls, trellises, fences, in shrubs and trees, and other climbing areas.

This old-fashioned hybrid is still the most popular clematis in gardens and is a parent of many of the more modern large-flowered varieties.

CLEMATIS, JACKMAN'S CLEMATIS

(Clematis x jackmanii)

Type: Perennial vine

Description: Cleome flowers, with many opening at once, grow in airy racemes 6 to 8 inches in diameter. Flowers—white, pink, or lavender in color—perch atop stems that grow up to 6 feet high.

How to grow: Cleomes grow well in average soil located in full sun or minimal shade. It is very drought-tolerant, although it will look and grow better if it is watered well. Space plants 1 to 3 feet apart.

Propagation: Sow after the last frost when the ground is warm. Cleomes may also be started indoors 4 to 6 weeks earlier at a temperature of at least 70°F. Germination time is 10 to 14 days. In the garden, it reseeds prolifically.

Uses: Plant cleome for its height, to back up borders, in the center of island beds, or in any spot where its dramatic quality stands out.

Related varieties: 'Helen Campbell' is a popular white variety. 'Rose Queen' is salmon-pink, and 'Ruby Queen' is rose-colored.

CLEOME, SPIDER FLOWER

(Cleome hasslerana)

Type: Annual

Exceedingly long stamens that extend well beyond the orchidlike flowers—somewhat resembling a daddy longlegs spider—are what give the spider flower its name.

Hardiness: Zones 3 to 8

Description: Single or bi-colored flowers float on top of a cluster of compound leaves. Flowers come in red, yellow, blue, purple, white, or a combination.

How to grow: Give columbines fertile, well-drained soil and full sun or partial shade. Many only live for a few years, so allow a few plants to self-sow for continued stock. To propagate, sow seeds in pots set outdoors. Seed from hybrids will not yield seedlings that resemble the parents.

Propagation: By seed

Uses: Columbines are excellent in beds and borders.

Related species and varieties: Many seed mixes are available. 'Songbird Mix' blooms are white with pink or purple. Wild columbine (*A. canadensis*) features red and yellow blooms.

COLUMBINE
(Aquilegia species)
Type: Perennial

Columbines are beloved by hummingbirds, are perfect for cut flowers, and have a long season of bloom.

CORALBELL
(Heuchera sanguinea)
Type: Perennial

Coralbells are American wildflowers originally from New Mexico and Arizona.

Hardiness: Zone 4

Description: Coralbells have mounds of basal leaves that are rounded and lobed, rising from a thick rootstock. The flowers are tiny bells on 1- to 2-foot slender stems blooming from spring into summer.

How to grow: In areas of hot summers, these plants like a bit of shade, but usually they prefer as much sun as possible. Plant them in good, well-drained garden soil with a high humus content and kept moist. In winter, coralbells resent wet soil and often will die. Divide every three years to prevent crowding.

Propagation: By division in spring or by seed

Uses: Use in a border, or plant among rocks, rock walls, and in the rock garden. Coralbells are also good cut flowers.

COREOPSIS
(Coreopsis species)

Type: Perennial

Hardiness: Zones 4 to 9

Description: Coreopsis sport bright daisylike flowers on wiry stems up to 3 feet high. Plants bear single or double flowers in shades of yellow, orange, pink, or white and have lance-shape, oval, or threadlike leaves.

How to grow: Coreopsis are happy in almost any well-drained garden soil in full sun. They are drought-resistant and an outstanding choice for hot, difficult places.

Propagation: By division in spring or by seed

Uses: Excellent for the wild garden and in the formal border, these flowers are prized for cutting. The smaller types are also good for edging plants. Coreopsis are well suited for patio containers and hanging baskets.

Related species and varieties: *C. verticillata* 'Moonbeam' has pale yellow daisies, and 'Zagreb' has deep yellow ones. 'Early Sunrise' blooms the first year from seed and produces double yellow flowers.

Over 100 species of coreopsis exist. Most of the commonly used varieties are very long bloomers and are some of the easiest perennials to care for.

Cosmos is one of the fastest-growing annuals. Some varieties reach up to 6 feet by summer's end.

COSMOS
(Cosmos bipinnatus)

Type: Annual

Description: Cosmos forms a lacy, open plant with flowers 3 to 4 inches in diameter. These "daisies" come in pink, red, white, and lavender with a contrasting yellow center.

How to grow: Cosmos grows best in full sun, but it will bloom acceptably in partial shade. Space at least 12 inches apart.

Propagation: Because it grows so fast, sow outdoors after danger of frost has passed. Barely cover seeds; they need light to germinate. Germination takes 3 to 7 days at 70° to 75°F.

Uses: Cosmos should be planted at the back of borders and grouped against fences or other places as a covering.

Related species and varieties: *C. bipinnatus* 'Sea Shells' features flowers with pretty rolled petals. *C. sulphureus* grows 1 to 3 feet tall and produces orange, red, or yellow blooms.

DAFFODIL

(Narcissus)

Type: Bulb

Hardiness: Zones 3 to 8

Description: Daffodils are bulbous perennials that bloom in early spring. Flowers appear singly or in clusters atop stems that range in height from 6 inches to 18 inches or more. Daffodils generally feature a trumpet-like cup or crown surrounded by 6 petals, in colors ranging from white to yellow to orange to pink to bi-colors. Many varieties readily produce more than one stalk. All bear similar strap-like leaves that fade away in late spring.

How to grow: Plant large bulbs 8 inches deep and 6 inches apart in a sunny, well-drained spot. Small bulbs can be planted only 4 inches deep and much more closely. Plant in early fall.

Propagation: By division after leaves fade in spring

Uses: Cut flowers, beds, and naturalizing. Small varieties are ideal in rock gardens.

Related species and varieties: Daffodils are divided into several categories, including trumpet daffodils (yellow-flowered King Alfred is the typical cut flower daffodil), large-cupped narcissi, small-cupped narcissi, multi-flowering Tazetta narcissi, and others.

Narcissus poeticus have pure white petals surrounding a crinkled cup. Cups are typically yellow and rimmed with red.

Narcissus tazetta have fragrant flowers with 3 or more blooms per stem.

Daffodils make cheery vase arrangements, either by themselves or mixed with other flowers.

Hardiness: Zones 8 to 11

Description: Dahlias grow from 1 to 5 feet tall. Flowers come in every color except blue, and the form is varied: peonylike; anemone-flowered; singles; shaggy mops; formal, ball-shaped; and twisted, curled petals. The flowers are carried on long stems above the erect plants. The American Dahlia Society has classified dahlias by both type and size. There are 12 different flower types: single, anemone-flowered, collarette, peony-flowered, formal decorative, informal decorative, ball, pompon, incurved cactus, straight cactus, semi-cactus, and orchid-flowered.

DAHLIA
(*Dahlia* hybrids)
Type: Bulb

From huge, dinner-plate-sized blooms down to midget pompons only 2 inches in diameter, dahlias show as much diversity as any summer flowering plant.

Semi-cactus dahlias

'Apple Blossom' is a collarette dahlia cultivar.

How to grow: Give dahlias full sun and rich, moist, well-drained soil. Plant outdoors after danger of frost has passed. Full-size dahlias reach 6 feet tall and need staking. Dwarf types are 12 to 18 inches tall and can sprawl. Grow dahlias from clumps of tuberous roots, or sow seeds indoors.

Propagation: Most of the large-flowered varieties are grown from tuberous roots available at garden centers or specialist growers. At the end of a summer's growing season, dig clumps of tubers and store in a cool but frost-free location until spring. Sow dahlia seeds 4 to 6 weeks prior to planting out at 70°F. Germination will take 5 to 14 days.

Uses: Full-size dahlias are useful at the back of borders. Dwarf types work well as edging or in containers. Dahlias, especially long stemmed types, make good cut flowers. Flowers with short stems or no stems at all may be floated in a bowl of water.

Related varieties: There are hundreds of varieties; consult your garden center or a specialist grower.

DAMASK ROSE

(Rosa damascena)

Type: Shrub

The Damask rose is well-known for its intoxicating fragrance.

Description: The Damask rose (*Rosa damascena*) is a rose hybrid derived from *Rosa gallica* and *Rosa moschata*. This is a hardy, deciduous shrub growing 4 feet tall. Colors range from whites and creams to soft pinks and a rare red. The blossoms tend to be smaller, often measuring less than 2 inches across.

How to grow: Damask rose shrubs tend to have sprawling growth habits and sharp thorns. Space about 4 to 6 feet apart, closer when grown as hedges.

Propagation: Most shrub roses can be readily multiplied by division or cuttings.

Uses: Shrub roses are unrivalled for use in privacy hedges and shrub borders, and many are excellent in seashore plantings. The Damask rose is also a commercial crop thanks to its sweet, intense scent. It is the source of attar of roses, which is the basis for many shampoos and perfumes.

Bottom right: The Damask rose is one of the oldest rose varieties. Today, Bulgaria and Turkey are the largest producers of *Rosa damascena* cultivars. Kazanlak, Bulgaria, is particularly well-known for its cultivation of Damask roses.

Bottom left: 'Celsiana Roses,' a related variety, bear semi-double, pale pink flowers with ruffled petals, and a delightful fragrance.

The scientific name of the wild daylily is *Hemerocallis fulva*. *Hemero* means "beautiful" and *callis* "day" in Greek. Each individual blossom opens, matures, and then withers in 24 hours or less.

DAYLILY
(Hemerocallis fulva)
Type: Perennial

Hardiness: Zones 3 to 9

Description: Daylilies have tuberous and fleshy roots with mostly basal, sword-shape leaves. The leaves usually grow up to 2 feet long with tall, multibranched stalks, each containing many 6-petaled lily-like flowers. Once blooming only in summer, new varieties called rebloomers begin to bloom in May and continue blooming into September.

How to grow: Give daylilies full sun and average, well-drained soil. They tolerate drought and damp soil. Plants benefit from partial shade in the South.

Propagation: By division in spring or fall

Uses: Entire gardens can be created using these marvelous plants, or they can be interspersed with other perennials. By mixing early, mid-, and late season blooming types, daylilies can bloom from late spring to fall.

DIANTHUS, PINK, CARNATION
(Dianthus species)
Type: Perennial, biennial

Hardiness: Zones 3 to 10

Description: These popular flowers bloom in shades of pink, red, white, orange, purple, or cranberry. Blooms range from less than an inch to several inches wide. Height varies from just a few inches to several feet.

How to grow: Give plants full or nearly full sun and average to rich, well-drained soil. Some cultivars must grow from cuttings or division, while others can grow from seed. Germination requirements vary; follow seed package directions.

Uses: Grow in beds, rock gardens, and containers.

Dianthus barbatus, or sweet william, is a biennial, but self-seeding produces new flowering plants year after year.

DUSTY MILLER, SILVER RAGWORT

(Jacobaea maritima)

Type: Perennial

Hardiness: 7b to 10b

Description: *Jacobaea maritima* (formerly known as *Senecio cineraria*) is a perennial plant often treated as a half-hardy annual. Dusty miller rarely flowers with yellow blossoms. It is grown for its silver-gray, feltlike foliage.

How to grow: Dusty miller prefers full sun and a rather ordinary, well-drained soil, although they will brighten lightly shaded areas, too. Plant in the garden when the soil has warmed and after danger of frost has passed. Space 8 to 10 inches apart.

Propagation: By seed or by cuttings. Germinate seeds at 75° to 80°F. Germination will take 10 to 15 days. Sow seeds 12 to 14 weeks before planting outside.

Uses: Dusty miller are effective in all kinds of planters. They also make great ribbons of light in flower beds and borders.

The name "dusty miller" has been commonly applied to a variety of similar silvery plants.

Dusty miller adds interesting texture to flower arrangements and bouquets.

ECHINACEA, PURPLE CONEFLOWER

(Echinacea purpurea)

Type: Perennial

Hardiness: Zones 3 to 10

Description: Also called purple coneflower, this heat-tolerant native produces daisylike flowers with prickly, cone-shape centers and rose-purple, white, yellow, or orange petals (ray flowers) on stout stalks standing 2 to 4 feet high. Leaves are alternate, simple, and coarse.

How to grow: Drought-tolerant coneflowers will grow in almost any well-drained garden soil in full sun. They grow well in partial shade in warmer regions. If soil is too rich, the flowers may need staking. Remove spent flowers to prolong blooming.

Propagation: By division in spring or by seed

Uses: Use coneflowers in beds and borders or in sunny wildflower gardens. They make excellent cut flowers.

This American native was once found naturally from Ohio to Iowa and south to Louisiana and Georgia.

Breeding and selection have added semi-doubles and doubles to the array of available English daisy varieties.

Description: English daisies have white, pink, or red flowers. Single and semi-double flowers are centered in yellow, but this distinguishing feature is covered in fully double varieties. Normally, flowers are 1 to 2 inches in diameter; newer varieties are larger. Most flowers appear in spring and early summer repeating again in the fall, but in cool and coastal climates they may bloom all year.

How to grow: Although a perennial, the English daisy is typically grown as a biennial in the South or as an annual in the North. Grow in full sun or light shade in moist soil, well-enriched with organic matter. When used as an annual, set out large seedlings as early as the ground can be worked or plant in the fall for earliest bloom when weather warms (except in zones 3 to 5 where they are not hardy). Plant roughly 6 to 9 inches apart.

Propagation: By seed or by division. Seeds germinate in 10 to 15 days at 70°F.

Uses: English daisies will liven up small beds and are good for edgings and small containers during the cool spring period.

ENGLISH DAISY

(Bellis perennis)

Type: Annual, biennial, perennial

False indigo was originally planted to produce a blue dye for early American colonists. It is a beautiful plant in leaf, in flower, and after going to seed.

Hardiness: Zone 3

Description: This large plant grows to 4 feet in height. The blue-green, compound leaves on stout stems are attractive all summer; and the dark blue, pealike flowers that eventually become blackened pods are very showy.

How to grow: False indigo needs well-drained soil in full sun, but will accept some partial shade. Being a member of the legume family, *baptisia* will do well in poor soil. The root systems of older plants become so extensive that they are difficult to move.

Propagation: By division or by seed

Uses: False indigo is a wonderful addition to cottage, prairie, and native plant gardens.

FALSE INDIGO, WILD INDIGO

(Baptisia australis)

Type: Perennial

FLOSS FLOWER, AGERATUM

(Ageratum houstonianum)

Type: Annual

Description: These fluffy flowers bloom continuously from summer to fall in shades of blue-lavender, white, or pink.

How to grow: Grow in any well-drained soil in full sun or partial shade. Space 6 to 10 inches apart for solid color. Occasional deadheading improves performance.

Propagation: Start seeds indoors 6 to 8 weeks before planting. Move plants outdoors after all chance of frost has passed. Cover seeds very lightly; they need some light to germinate well. Seeds germinate in 5 to 8 days at 70°F.

Uses: Plant compact, mounding types, 6 to 10 inches high, in the front of borders and beds. Use 12- to 15-inch-tall selections for cut flowers.

Related species and varieties: Several of the popular blue varieties are 'Adriatic,' 'Blue Danube,' and 'Blue Blazer.' Golden ageratum, or *Lonas inodora*, has the same flower effect in bright yellow.

Forget-me-nots are small, blue, five-petaled flowers with yellow or white eyes.

FORGET-ME-NOT
(Myosotis sylvatica)

Type: Annual, biennial

Description: Forget-me-nots are biennials that are usually grown as annuals. They seldom reach more than 12 inches in height and equal in diameter. The tiny flowers are clustered together in racemes at the top of plants.

How to grow: Forget-me-nots relish cool, moist weather with sun or partial shade. In zones 8 to 10, you can sow seeds in the fall where plants will bloom in the spring. When planting in spring, plant as soon as soil can be worked. When plants have finished blooming, replace them with summer annuals. Forget-me-nots will reseed, but seedlings in colder climates will not bloom until late spring or summer.

Propagation: By seed. For early bloom in cold climates, seed indoors in January, planting seedlings outdoors as soon as soil warms. Seeds germinate in 8 to 14 days at 55° to 70°F. Cover seeds; they need darkness. When removing plants that have bloomed, shake the ripened seeds onto the ground where you want blooming plants the next spring.

Uses: Plant in masses for best results. They're suited for rock gardens, as an edging, or in front of a border plant. Try them in window boxes and patio planters with spring bulbs.

Biennials native to cool, moist areas of Europe and northern Asia, forget-me-nots are usually grown as annuals.

FOXGLOVE

(Digitalis purpurea)

Type: Biennial, perennial

Hardiness: Zones 4 to 9

Description: Foxgloves produce gray-green leaves topped by 2- to 5-foot-tall, bloom-heavy stalks in early summer. The tubular, bell-shape flowers come in shades of pink, purple-pink, white, or creamy yellow, generally with a contrasting color speckling their throats.

How to grow: Give foxgloves light shade and average, moist, well-drained soil. Afternoon shade is important in hot climates. To grow foxgloves as biennials, sow seeds outdoors in pots in June or July, and transplant to the garden in fall.

Propagation: By seed. For bloom the first year, sow indoors 8 to 10 weeks prior to planting outdoors. Except for selected varieties, these will bloom in late summer or fall. Seeds germinate in 15 to 20 days at 70°F.

Uses: Plant foxgloves at the back of borders, against fences, near shrubs, or along woodlands. They make useful cut flowers. Because the plants are poisonous, keep out of reach of young children and pets.

Digitalis grandiflora, commonly called yellow foxglove, is a clump-forming perennial with large, tubular, yellow flowers with interior brown markings.

A widely used heart medicine comes from this biennial plant, but its garden value is due to the spikes of bell-shaped flowers in late spring.

Hardiness: Zone 6

Description: Gaura has alternate, lance-shaped leaves up to 3 inches long on stout stems. It blooms with 1-inch, white, four-petaled flowers that persist throughout the summer. Stems can reach 6 feet.

How to grow: Gauras need full sun in good, deep, well-drained garden soil because the tap root is very long. They are both drought- and heat-resistant.

Propagation: By division in spring or by seed

Uses: Perfect for both a dry garden and a wild garden, gauras are also very attractive in a formal border. In northern climates, they bloom late in the season and are charming when planted with aster and ornamental grasses.

Right: There are a number of gauras that are native American wildflowers; however, this particular species is the best for the garden. Found naturally from Louisiana to Texas and south to Mexico, the white flowers will slowly fade to pink as they age.

GAURA
(Gaura lindheimeri)
Type: Perennial

Gaura lindheimeri typically blooms from August to October. Gauras work well when planted in groups in wildflower gardens.

This South African flower likes hot, dry summers. Gardeners treasure it for its daisylike flowers.

GAZANIA, TREASURE FLOWER
(Gazania rigens)
Type: Annual, perennial

Description: Grown for their brilliantly colored, daisylike flowers, gazanias are 8 to 12 inches tall and sport blooms in white, pink, bronze, red, yellow, or orange. Many selections feature petals with multiple contrasting colors.

How to grow: Plant gazanias in full sun and poor to average, well-drained soil. They tolerate drought, heat, and salt spray. Grow them as perennials from zone 8 south. To grow as annuals, start seed indoors.

Propagation: Sow seeds outdoors after final frost or plant them indoors 4 to 6 weeks earlier. Seeds germinate in 15 to 20 days at 70°F. Cuttings taken in the summer root quickly.

Uses: Plant gazanias in the front of beds and borders. Use them as a ground cover in sunny, dry areas or in rock gardens.

Related varieties: Daybreak series blooms in 'Yellow,' 'Orange,' and 'Garden Sun,' combining yellow and orange. 'Daybreak Mixture' includes pink and white colors.

Left: *Gazania rigens var. leucolaena* is a trailing gazania commonly used as ground cover. Cultivars of this variety include 'Sunburst,' 'Sunglow,' and 'Sunrise Yellow.'

Right: This variety of gazania flower has white petals streaked with purple.

Description: Bushy tender perennials commonly grown as annuals, geraniums bear showy clusters of flowers in shades of red, pink, salmon, or white. Plants bloom from late spring to frost. Scented geraniums have aromatic leaves but less-showy blooms.

How to grow: Give geraniums full sun and average to rich soil that's well drained. Deadhead to remove spent flowers. Start with plants or cuttings, or grow from seeds sown indoors 10 to 12 weeks before the last spring frost date.

Propagation: By seed or by cuttings. Cuttings root easily. Make cuttings 8 to 10 weeks prior to planting out for husky plants. Seed-grown varieties should be started 10 to 12 weeks prior to garden planting. Seeds germinate in 7 to 10 days at 70° to 75°F.

Uses: All geraniums make excellent container plants. Ivy-leaf geraniums (*Pelargonium peltatum*) are particularly attractive in hanging baskets, window boxes, and patio planters. Zonal geraniums (*Pelargonium x hortorum*) are among the best plants for formal beds. They can provide pockets of color in any sunny spot. Put scented geraniums any place where you can partake of their fragrance frequently.

Related species and varieties: In spring, garden centers stock a multitude of cultivars in a wide range of colors and bloom types.

Many gardeners consider zonal geraniums (*Pelargonium x hortorum*) the epitome of summer flowers. These stalwart garden beauties are tender perennials that must be replanted each year except in the most favored climates.

GERANIUM
(*Pelargonium* species)
Type: Annual, tender perennial

A majority of *Pelargonium* species come from South Africa, but through hundreds of years of breeding, the parentage of today's varieties has been obscured.

Description: Globe amaranths bear 1-inch-wide, papery-textured, cloverlike flowers all summer long; blooms come in violet, lavender, red, orange, pink, or creamy white. Plants can grow up to 2 feet tall. Newer, smaller varieties are bushy dwarfs.

How to grow: Give globe amaranths full sun and any well-drained soil. Plant in the garden after the last frost and space 10 to 15 inches apart.

Propagation: Soak seeds in water for 3 to 4 days before sowing. Sow seeds in place in the garden after the last frost date. Seeds germinate in 14 to 21 days at 65° to 75°F.

Uses: Mix globe amaranths with other flowers in beds and borders. Use dwarf varieties for edging beds, borders, or as a colorful ground cover. Grow extra plants for cutting and drying.

Related varieties: Dwarf 'Purple Buddy' is 9 to 12 inches tall. 'Strawberry Fields' is bright red. Several mixes are also available.

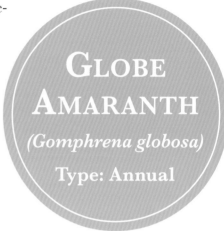

GLOBE AMARANTH
(Gomphrena globosa)
Type: Annual

This tropical native has small, cloverlike flowers that will continually bloom throughout the whole summer season.

Hardiness: Zone 3

Description: Thick, rounded evergreen leaves, often 1 foot long, grow from a single crown and are edged with red in cold weather. Flowers are pink with waxy petals, which bloom in drooping clusters.

How to grow: These plants prefer light shade and good, moist soil with plenty of organic matter.

Propagation: By division or by seed

Uses: Excellent as an edging in the border or planted in groups on slopes, bergenias are also a fine addition to the rock garden. Bergenias are also good cut flowers.

HEARTLEAF BERGENIA
(Bergenia cordifolia)
Type: Perennial

Bergenias trace their origins from Siberia and Mongolia. As such they are perfectly happy in low temperatures when covered with snow.

HELIOTROPE, CHERRY PIE
(Heliotropium arborescens)
Type: Annual

Description: Heliotrope has long, gray-green leaves with deep veins; reaching a height of 1 foot with an equal spread is reasonable. Many tiny flowers are clustered in the large heads carried well above the foliage.

How to grow: Any good garden soil with medium fertility in full sun will grow good heliotropes. Normally, plants are started early indoors (from seeds or cuttings) and transplanted outdoors when danger of frost has passed and the ground is warm. Depending on the size of transplants, space from 8 to 15 inches apart.

Propagation: Sow seeds 10 to 12 weeks before planting out. Seeds germinate in 7 to 21 days at 70° to 85°F. Root the cuttings in four-inch pots in February in order to have husky plants for May planting.

Uses: Tuck heliotropes into rock gardens, or grow them in the front of borders.

Fragrance is one of the most alluring attributes of heliotropes. Flowers bloom in copious quantities of deep blue, violet, lavender, or white during the summer.

HIBISCUS, ROSE MALLOW, SWAMP MALLOW
(Hibiscus moscheutos)
Type: Perennial

Hardiness: Zones 5 to 10

Description: This native American wildflower bears flowers up to 10 inches across in shades of pink, red, or white. The shrub-size plants bloom for much of the summer and form tough clumps that can reach 8 feet in height.

How to grow: Give plants full sun to light shade and moist, average to rich soil. Buy plants, or start from seed. Growth emerges late in spring, so it's wise to mark the locations of clumps.

Propagation: By division or by seed

Uses: Use mallows in wild gardens, in areas with damp soil, or toward the back of a bed or border.

Related species and varieties: Numerous hybrids are suitable for adding a tropical flair to gardens. 'Southern Belle' produces huge flowers in red, rose, pink, and white and grows to 4 feet tall. 'Lord Baltimore' bears red flowers and reaches 8 feet in height.

Hardiness: Zones 3 to 9

Description: Old-fashioned garden favorites, hollyhocks have upright stalks covered with showy, single or double flowers. Blooms come in shades of pink, white, red, maroon, or yellow. Each flower is 2 to 4 inches wide. Full-size plants reach heights of 4 to 6 feet or more; dwarf types range from 2 to 3 feet.

How to grow: Plant in full sun and average, well-drained soil. Stake tall selections on windy sites. Replace plants every other year to minimize diseases such as rust. Plants self-sow, but seedlings may not resemble their parents.

Propagation: By seed. Sow seeds indoors or outside in individual pots to minimize transplant stress. Germination takes 10 to 24 days at 70°F.

Uses: Plant standard hollyhocks along fences or buildings or toward the rear of flower gardens.

HOLLYHOCK

(Alcea rosea)

Type: Biennial, perennial

Hollyhocks are the quintessential cottage garden flower. Although they are short-lived biennials, hollyhocks are once again popular in American gardens.

HYBRID TEA ROSE

Type: Shrub

Single-stemmed, large-flowered, and delicately perfumed, hybrid teas are the epitome of the perfect rose.

Description: Hybrid tea roses generally bear one flower at the end of each stem. A signature of hybrid teas is the long, pointed buds that open delicately into a delightful flower. The color range is the most complete among roses. Plants generally reach about 3 feet in height in cold climates and up to 5 feet in warmer ones.

How to grow: Space 24 to 30 inches apart in cold climates; 3 to 4 feet in warm ones. Hybrid teas need harsher pruning than most other roses. They tend to suffer from severe winter kill, and full winter protection is necessary in cold regions. Remove faded flowers to ensure continual bloom.

Propagation: Few hybrid teas grow well on their own roots. They are usually sold in the form of grafted plants.

Uses: The "long-stemmed roses" of the florist industry are hybrid teas. Since their growing habit tends to be rigidly upright and rather sparse, they are best planted in the center of beds where their flowers, rather than their overall appearance, will be noticed.

Hardiness: Zones 3 to 9

Description: Hydrangeas have been treasured garden plants for decades. *Hydrangea arborescens*, also known as smooth hydrangea or wild hydrangea, is a deciduous shrub that typically grows 3 to 6 feet tall and spreads just as wide. The plant flowers from June through September, sometimes later. The blooms start a light green color, then turn creamy/bright white as the flower matures. Leaves are ovate (egg-shaped), toothed, and pointed.

How to grow: Most hydrangeas adapt to a wide range of growing conditions. *Hydrangea arborescens* prefers organically rich, moist, well-drained soil and partial shade. They can only tolerate full sun if given consistent moisture. This hydrangea is often treated as an herbaceous perennial and pruned back to the ground in winter.

Propagation: By seed or by cuttings

Uses: Group *Hydrangea arborescens* in partially shaded areas of the mixed shrub border, woodland garden, or as background for a perennial border. Hydrangeas also make nice cut flowers.

Related species and varieties: 'Annabelle' is one of the best-known and most cold hardy cultivars of *Hydrangea arborescens*. The flowers of bigleaf hydrangea, or *Hydrangea macrophylla*, change color depending on the soil pH—blue in highly acidic soils and lilac to pink in slightly acidic to alkaline soils. Climbing hydrangea (*Hydrangea anomala petiolaris*) slowly scales its support and doesn't need to be pruned unless it outgrows its space.

Hydrangea arborescens is native to the eastern United States, from New York to Florida and west to Louisiana and Oklahoma.

HYDRANGEA, SMOOTH HYDRANGEA

(Hydrangea arborescens)

Type: Shrub

Mophead or bigleaf hydrangea (*Hydrangea macrophylla*), change flower color depending on the acidity of the soil: blue in acidic soil, pink in alkaline. Mopheads have large, round flower clusters.

IMPATIENS
(Impatiens species)
Type: Annual

Description: Glorious shade-garden plants, impatiens are mounding, 12- to 15-inch-tall annuals that are covered with flowers from summer to frost. Single or double flowers come in white, pink, rose, orange, scarlet, burgundy, or lavender, with many variants.

How to grow: Give impatiens partial shade to shade and average, well-drained soil. Bloom diminishes in deep shade. Start with plants, or sow seeds indoors 10 to 12 weeks before the last spring frost date.

Propagation: By seed or by cuttings. Germination takes 10 to 20 days at 75°F. Cuttings root in 10 to 14 days.

Uses: Grow impatiens as edging, as ground cover, or in colorful drifts added to shady beds and borders. Dwarf types are especially effective in containers.

Related species and varieties: There are many mixes that offer a variety of colors. African hybrids have orchidlike blooms; New Guinea impatiens bear large flowers, 2 to 3 inches across.

Impatiens flower in almost all colors. Their tidy mounding habit makes them ideal low-maintenance plants.

This large genus contains more than 200 species in the northern hemisphere and is most abundant in Asia. The plants are responsible for a marvelous array of flowers plus, in many cases, fine foliage. The blue flags, *Iris versicolor* or *I. prismatica*, are lovely wildflowers from the Northeast.

Hardiness: Zone 3 and above

Description: Irises usually have basal leaves in two ranks—linear to sword-shaped—often resembling a fan, arising from a thick rootstock (or rhizome) or, in some species, from a bulb. They bloom in shades of pink, blue, lilac, purple to brown, yellow, orange, almost black, and white. There are no true reds.

How to grow: Most irises need sunlight. Except for those like the water flag (*Iris pseudacorus*), which delights in a watery spot, or the Japanese iris (*I. ensata*), which thrives in a humus-rich, moist soil, most irises also prefer a good, well-drained garden soil.

Propagation: By division in the fall or by seed

Uses: Even though the bloom period is short, a bed of irises is ideal for a flower garden. There are irises for the poolside and the pool, the wild or woodland garden, the early spring bulb bed, and the rock garden.

IRIS
(Iris species)
Type: Hardy perennial

LARKSPUR, ANNUAL DELPHINIUM

(Consolida ajacis)

Type: Annual

Description: Larkspur grows up to 4 feet tall with delphinium-like flowers, single or double, evenly spaced around the long stem above lacy, gray-green foliage. Although blue is favored, larkspur also flowers in pink, salmon, rose, lavender, purple, and white.

How to grow: Grow in moist, well-drained soil in full sun. Larkspur exposed to high winds may need staking. It performs best in cool weather. Remove spent blossoms to encourage new blooms. Larkspur is poisonous, so be careful planting them where pets and children are present.

Propagation: Sow seeds in place because larkspur does not transplant well. Sow in the fall or as soon as ground can be worked in spring. For summer and fall blooms in cool climates, successively sow 2 to 3 weeks apart until mid-May.

Uses: Groups of larkspur backing informal annuals can give a cottage garden look. Cluster them at the side or at the back of the flower border or center them in island beds to lend height. They're good cut flowers and may be dried for winter bouquets.

This aromatic herb originally hails from the Mediterranean. The genus name, which comes from a Latin word meaning "to wash," alludes to the ancient custom of scenting bath water with lavender.

Hardiness: Zones 5 to 8

Description: Richly fragrant lavender is an aromatic herb that bears terminal clusters of lavender, dark purple, pink, or white flowers in summer. The gray-green, evergreen leaves are as fragrant as the flowers. Plants are 2 to 3 feet tall and shrubby.

How to grow: Lavender plants want full sun and well-drained, average to sandy soil. Plants are quite drought tolerant once established and also tolerate light shade. In the spring, prune back the deadwood, and shape the plants. Start with plants, or sow seeds outdoors in pots.

Propagation: By soft cuttings in spring or by seed

Uses: Grow lavender in beds and borders, as low hedges, in herb gardens, or in rock gardens. Dry the fragrant flowers and use in sachets and potpourris.

LAVENDER

(Lavandula angustifolia)

Type: Perennial

Lilies are the mainstay of the summer bulb garden. Although each species has a relatively short blooming period, with careful selection it is possible to have a garden filled with nothing but lilies from early summer until mid-fall.

LILY
(*Lilium* species)
Type: Bulb

Hardiness: Zones 3 to 8

Description: There is a wide variety of lilies, and a concise description of the whole group is difficult. Generally, they bear large trumpet-shaped flowers that can face upward, outward, or downward. The latter are often called Turk's cap lilies. Lilies come in just about every color but true blue, and many are attractively spotted or mottled. Stems are usually upright and covered with grasslike leaves and range in height from a few inches to 7 feet or more.

How to grow: Buy only fresh bulbs and plant as soon as possible since lily bulbs never go entirely dormant and cannot tolerate drying out. Plant bulbs 4 to 8 inches deep (2 inches for *Lilium candidum*) and up to 1 foot apart in either late fall or spring. The ideal site is in rich, well-drained soil with humus. The plants need plenty of sun yet some protection from midday rays. Mulching is recommended.

Propagation: By division or bulb scales. Species lilies can be grown from seed.

Uses: Dwarf lilies can be placed in the front of the border, but most others look best toward the middle or back of the garden. Many are readily naturalized in meadows or on the edge of wooded areas. All make excellent cut flowers. Do not cut too much foliage when harvesting the flowers, or the bulb will weaken.

Related species and varieties: Asiatic hybrids are early flowering; Aurelian hybrids bloom in midsummer; and Oriental hybrids are late blooming. Species lilies include the classic Madonna (*Lilium candidum*), with white flowers, and the Regal (*L. regale*), white with a yellow center and lilac-pink exterior.

Left: Casablanca lilies are popular in flower gardens and bridal bouquets.

Right: Tiger lilies bear orange blooms with dark spots.

Description: Also called prairie gentian, this plant is native from the Midwest to Mexico and bears somewhat poppylike, cup-shape flowers in bluish-purple, blue, pink, or white. Plants grow up to 3 feet tall. Although most are single-flowered, semi-double and double-flowered selections are available.

How to grow: Give lisianthus full sun and rich, moist soil. To grow them as annuals, sow seeds 3 months before the last spring frost date. Use individual pots, since they have taproots and are difficult to transplant. Germination takes 10 to 20 days at 75° to 80°F. Pinch out the growing tips to induce branching and greater flowering.

Uses: Grow lisianthus in cutting gardens, beds, and containers. Their rose-like appearance makes them a popular pick for flower arrangements.

Related varieties: Many mixes are available. Single-color offerings are great as cut flowers and for landscape effect.

Though it will survive winters in USDA zones 8 to 10, lisianthus is best grown as an annual.

LISIANTHUS
(Eustoma grandiflorum)

Type: Annual

The American marigold (*Tagetes erecta*), also called African or Aztec marigold, comes in such an array of bright colors over a long season that they're a mainstay of gardeners everywhere.

Description: Cheerful marigolds range from 8 inches to 3 feet in height and bear single to fully double flowers in yellow, gold, orange, or creamy white. French marigolds (*Tagetes patula*) are bushier and more compact than American types (*Tagetes erecta*), which have larger flowers.

How to grow: Marigolds grow best in full sun with moist, well-drained soil, although they will tolerate drier conditions. Start with plants, or sow seeds indoors. Seeds germinate in 5 to 7 days at 65° to 75°F. Move transplants to the garden as soon as all danger of frost has passed. Space French marigolds 6 to 10 inches apart; Americans 10 to 18 inches apart.

Uses: Grow taller types toward the center or rear of beds and borders. Use French marigolds as edging and in containers.

Related varieties: Hundreds of color and form variations are available. Plant a mix or a single color, depending on your garden design.

MARIGOLD
(Tagetes species)

Type: Annual

Description: The moon flower is a close relative of the morning glory, and produces a long, twining vine that can grow more than 12 feet high over the course of a year. Moon flower vines often climb up and over fences, shrubs, and various other stationary backdrops. Moon flower vines always coil clockwise.

How to grow: Moon flower plants grow rapidly from seed. They form large, heart-shaped leaves that can reach up to 6 inches across. The moon flower blooms most easily in late summer and early fall, as long as its surroundings are not too dry. The delicate white blooms are solitary and are usually 5 to 6 inches across. Each moon flower blossom is marked by a narrow, five-pointed star in varying shades of white.

Uses: Moon flowers are good for trellises, fences, and such. Its blossoms are beautiful and add elegance to any outdoor garden.

MOON FLOWER
(Ipomoea alba)
Type: Vine

The moon flower has large, fragrant, white flowers that open in the evening and close before midday. It is a garden essential for those who enjoy nighttime gardening.

'Heavenly Blue' is a popular cultivar of *Ipomoea*.

Description: These easy-to-grow, dependable vines bear trumpet-shape blooms in true blue, purple, pink, crimson red, or white, with many bi-color combinations available. Blooms open from dawn to midmorning, each lasting only a day. Plants have heart-shaped leaves and reach 10 feet in height/length.

How to grow: Give morning glories full sun and average soil. Soak seeds in water a day before planting. Sow outdoors when all danger of frost has passed or indoors 4 to 6 weeks before the last spring frost. Germination takes a week at 70°F. Plants need a trellis or other support on which to climb.

Uses: Plant along fences, trellises, or shrubs that they can climb.

Related species and varieties: 'Heavenly Blue' is a rich blue heirloom. 'Scarlett O'Hara' bears crimson red flowers. Related convolvulus (*Convolvulus tricolor*) produces bushy, 14-inch plants with pink, blue, purple, or rose morning-glory-type flowers.

MORNING GLORY
(Ipomoea species)
Type: Annual vine

Except for the roots, all parts of nasturtium—including the leaves, buds, flowers, pods, and seeds—are edible. They add a peppery taste to salads.

NASTURTIUM
(Tropaeolum majus)
Type: Annual

Canary creeper (*Tropaeolum peregrinum*) is a species related to nasturtium.

Description: Nasturtiums bear nearly round leaves and yellow, red, maroon, or orange flowers. Flowers and foliage are edible and peppery tasting. Plants are either vinelike and 4 to 10 feet in length or about 12 inches tall and bushy.

How to grow: Give nasturtiums full sun and dry, sandy, well-drained soil. Cool, dry summers suit them best. Sow seeds outdoors after last spring frost, or start them in individual pots indoors 4 to 5 weeks before the last frost date. Tie vining types to supports; they have no means of attachment. Germination takes 10 to 14 days at 65° to 70°F.

Uses: Bushy types are good for borders, beds, and edging. Tie vining types to fences or trellises. Use either in containers.

Related species: *Tropaeolum peregrinum*, or canary creeper, is a vigorous vine with bright yellow flowers.

ORNAMENTAL ONION, FLOWERING ONION

(*Allium* species)

Type: Bulb

Hardiness: Zones 4 to 10

Description: Alliums bear spheres or loose clusters of star-shaped flowers in shades of pink, white, blue, purple, or yellow. There are both tall-growing species (to 4 feet or higher) and miniature ones. Their attractive leaves, often a lovely blue-green, appear in early spring but fade away in early summer, often just as the plant is flowering.

How to grow: Plant small bulbs 3 to 4 inches deep, large ones 6 to 8 inches deep, in a sunny, well-drained area. Winter mulching is advisable in colder climates.

Propagation: By division or by seed

Uses: Low-growing alliums are ideal plants for borders and rock gardens. Tall-growing alliums make wonderful cut flowers; soak their stems in cold water for 10 minutes to remove any scent of onion. They are also attractive in beds and borders of all sorts.

Related species: *Allium giganteum* produces 6-inch globes of purple flowers on 3- to 6-foot stems and may require staking. Drumstick allium (*A. sphaerocephalum*) bears 2-foot stems with smaller clusters of reddish-purple flowers. Blue garlic (*A. caeruleum*) is similar but with blue flowers. Yellow allium (*A. moly*) produces yellow flowers in loose clusters on 10-inch stems. *A. neapolitanum* is similar but with beautifully perfumed white flowers.

You can't use ornamental onions in your cooking, but these beautiful plants deserve a spot in your flower garden.

Allium caeruleum

Allium giganteum

Description: Low-growing, cool-season annuals, pansies produce flowers that are 2 to 5 inches across and come in a complete range of colors. Solid-color selections are available, but many feature facelike markings in bright contrasting colors.

How to grow: Give pansies full sun—partial shade in hot climates—and rich, moist soil. From zone 7 south, plant them in fall for winter to spring bloom. Elsewhere, plant in early spring as soon as the ground thaws. Shear leggy plants back halfway to force new growth and bloom. Buy plants, or start from seeds sown 6 to 8 weeks prior to planting outdoors. Seeds germinate in 10 to 15 days at 68°F.

Uses: Plant pansies anywhere you want spots of color.

PANSY
(Viola x wittrockiana)

Type: Annual

Bottom left: Pansies are suitable for the front of borders and beds, in small groups among other flowers, in cottage garden plantings, and in containers.

Bottom right: The largest pansies of all are in the Super Majestic Giant series. Majestic Giants, shown here, are somewhat smaller.

Hardiness: Zones 7 to 9

Description: The genus *Passiflora* contains over 500 species of perennials, annuals, and even trees. Most are perennial vines, including *Passiflora caerulea*, commonly called blue passionflower. *P. caerulea* is a twining vine that grows up to 30 feet. It is evergreen in tropical climates, but deciduous where winters are cool. The 3- to 4-inch flowers, produced throughout the summer, have whitish petals and numerous blue-purple filaments that fan out from the center.

How to grow: Plant in full sun to partial shade in a rich, deep, moist, well-drained sandy loam. Prune heavily to remove deadwood and to control excess growth.

Uses: Where they are hardy, passionflowers are good for trellises, fences, pergolas, and the like. Where they are not hardy, passionflowers are often grown in pots and moved indoors over winter.

Related species and varieties: *P. coccinea*, commonly called red passionflower or red granadilla, is a tropical vine with red flowers. The purple passionflower (*P. incarnata*) grows to 8 feet with violet flowers; 'Alba' is a variety with white flowers.

PASSIONFLOWER
(*Passiflora* species)
Type: Vine

Passionflowers produce exotic, colorful blossoms, sometimes followed by brightly colored fruits. The plant's name comes from the complex structure of its flowers, each part of which can be seen as symbols of the crucifixion of Christ.

Purple passionflower (*Passiflora incarnata*) at the Butterfly Garden at Norfolk Botanical Garden, in Norfolk, Virginia

PEONY
(*Paeonia* species)
Type: Perennial

Hardiness: Zones 2 to 9

Description: Within the *Paeonia* genus, there are various species and cultivars. The most commonly planted species in North America is *Paeonia lactiflora*, sometimes called Chinese peony, an herbaceous perennial. Herbaceous peonies are shrubby plants with thick roots and large, compound, glossy green leaves on strong stems. They bear showy flowers with a pleasing fragrance. The blooms are followed by large, interesting seedpods. Flower forms include Japanese/anemone (single petals and obvious stamens); semi-double (double petals and showy center stamens that resemble petals); bomb double (many petals and rounded centers); and double (large petal-packed blooms). Herbaceous peonies die down to the ground for the winter. *Paeonia suffruticosa*, commonly called tree peony, is a deciduous, woody shrub. Like small trees, tree peonies remain in evidence all year and should not be cut down.

Most familiar peonies, such as this classic double pink 'Sarah Bernhardt,' are cultivars of the herbaceous species *Paeonia lactiflora*.

Left: 'Cardinal Vaughan' is an early-blooming tree peony bearing rich magenta flowers. Unlike herbaceous peonies, which die back to the ground in winter, tree peonies maintain their wood stems throughout the cold winter months.

Right: 'Bowl of Beauty' is an herbaceous peony featuring bowl-shaped blooms atop sturdy stems. The bright pink petals guard the narrow, cream-colored stamen filaments.

How to grow: Grow peonies in full sun (except in zones 8 and 9, where peonies may benefit from partial shade) and well-drained, moisture-retentive soil rich with humus. Plant bare-root peony plants in autumn. Some varieties need staking.

Propagation: By division, by cuttings, or by seed

Uses: As specimen plants, in hedges, beds, or borders, peonies should be an important part of any garden. Peonies also make excellent cut flowers—they're beautiful, fragrant, and long-lasting. Cut when not quite fully open to get the longest bloom from your cut peonies.

Description: Petunias come in different sizes and forms, but all bear showy, trumpet-shape flowers in shades of pink, lavender, purple, or red. Many bi-colors are available, too. Blooms may be single or double and range from about 2 to 4 inches wide.

How to grow: Full sun to light shade and average to rich, well-drained soil suit petunias best, although they tolerate poor soil. Deadhead regularly, and shear plants back halfway in midsummer to promote branching and more flowers. Start with plants, or sow seeds indoors 10 to 12 weeks before the last spring frost date. Seeds germinate in 10 to 12 days at 70° to 75°F.

Uses: Beds, borders, walkways, paths, containers—all will accommodate an abundance of petunias. Some varieties are especially recommended for containers, since they mound up and billow over the edges.

PETUNIA
(Petunia × hybrida)
Type: Annual

Hardiness: Zones 3 to 9

Description: Perennial phlox range from spring-blooming, 2-inch-high moss phlox (*P. subulata*) to 3- to 4-foot-tall garden phlox (*P. paniculata*), which bears showy clusters of fragrant flowers in summer. Blooms come in white, rose, pink, purple, lavender, blue, or magenta.

How to grow: Provide rich, moist, well-drained soil in full sun or light shade. Garden phlox is susceptible to powdery mildew, so buy disease-resistant cultivars and thin out stems in spring to improve air circulation. Divide clumps every 3 years to keep them vigorous. Propagate by division, or sow seeds. Sow annual phlox (*P. drummondii*) outdoors after last spring frost date, or start indoors 4 to 6 weeks earlier.

Uses: Grow garden phlox in borders. Low-growing species can be used in beds or as a ground cover.

PHLOX
(Phlox **species)**
Type: Annual, perennial

Phlox subulata is a spring-blooming creeping plant.

Phlox paniculata, commonly known as garden phlox or tall phlox, is a long-blooming perennial that grows in upright clumps.

Phlox drummondii is an annual phlox that is native to central and eastern Texas.

PINCUSHION FLOWER, SCABIOSA

(Scabiosa species)

Type: Perennial

Hardiness: Zones 3 to 8

Description: Pincushion flowers, or scabiosas, bear ruffled, buttonlike blooms in pink, violet, maroon, blue, or white. Plants are 1 to 2½ feet tall.

How to grow: Give plants full sun and average to rich, well-drained soil. Overly moist soil causes root rot. Sow seeds outdoors after the last spring frost date, or sow indoors 4 to 6 weeks before that date and move plants to the garden after danger of frost has passed. Seeds germinate in 10 to 15 days at 70° to 75°F. Deadhead to prolong bloom.

Uses: Grow in mixed beds and borders or in cottage gardens. Scabiosas also make excellent cut flowers that last for about 7 days in fresh arrangements.

Related species and varieties: *Scabiosa columbaria* is an outstanding, long-blooming perennial. 'Butterfly Blue' grows about 10 inches tall and bears light blue blooms. Starflower (*S. stellata*) makes a good dried flower.

Description: Gardeners grow poppies for their silky, crinkly petaled, early summer flowers. Oriental poppy (*Papaver orientale*) is a 2- to 4-foot-tall perennial with showy 4- to 6-inch-wide flowers. California poppy (*Eschscholzia californica*) bears 3-inch blooms on foot-tall plants in summer. For both, flowers come in a range of colors, including orange, pink, red, salmon, and white. California poppies also come in yellow.

P. orientale, or Oriental poppy, is a perennial plant typically grown in zones 3 to 7.

How to grow: Give poppies full sun and average, well-drained soil. Deadhead to reduce self-sowing. Sow California poppies outdoors in early spring; plant in fall in mild climates. Seeds germinate in 10 days at 60°F. Start perennial poppies from plants or seeds sown outdoors in pots.

Uses: Plant Oriental poppies among other flowers in beds or borders. Grow California poppies in rock walls or rock gardens or as part of naturalized meadow plantings.

California poppies or Golden poppies (*E. californica*) are treated as annuals in all but zones 8 to 10, where they perform like short-lived perennials.

POPPY

(Papaver and *Eschscholzia* species)

Type: Annual, perennial

Description: Also called moss rose and rose moss, this nearly prostrate annual bears an abundance of small flowers in jewellike colors, including yellow, gold, orange, crimson, pink, lavender, purple, and white. Blooms may be single or double and open in sunny weather.

How to grow: Portulacas need full sun and light, sandy, well-drained soil. They tolerate heat and drought but bloom better with adequate moisture. Sow seeds outdoors after the last spring frost date, or start indoors 4 to 6 weeks earlier. Either way, wait until the soil has warmed up to move plants or sow seed outdoors. Seeds germinate in 10 to 15 days at 70° to 80°F.

Uses: Grow portulaca as a ground cover or as edging on problem spots. They are notoriously good container plants that do not languish if you forget to water them one day.

PORTULACA, MOSS ROSE

(Portulaca grandiflora)

Type: Annual

Portulaca's profusion of sunny flower colors combined with its toughness make it a natural for difficult garden sites. It will do even better under less difficult conditions.

Salvias are dependable in any climate and adaptable to full sun or partial shade with equal ease. This species is *Salvia splendens*, also called Scarlet Sage.

Hardiness: Zones 4 to 9

Description: Grown for their showy spikes of small, two-lipped flowers, salvias come in red, pink, violet, lavender, blue, or white. Many feature fragrant foliage. Plants range from 8 inches to 4 or more feet tall, depending on the species. Hardiness varies, and many annual salvias are tender perennials that are hardy from zone 7 or 8 south. Overwinter these plants indoors in cold climates.

How to grow: Give plants full sun or partial shade and average, moist soil. Start with plants, or sow seeds indoors and move transplants to the garden after the danger of frost has passed. Seeds germinate in 12 to 15 days at 70° to 75°F.

Uses: Grow salvias in beds and borders. They also make good container plants.

Related species and varieties: 'Lady in Red' is an award-winning annual. 'Victoria' is a classic blue annual. 'Rose Queen' bears spikes of pink flowers.

SALVIA

(Salvia species)

Type: Annual, perennial

SNAPDRAGON
(Antirrhinum majus)
Type: Annual

Description: Best known for their two-lipped flowers that children love to snap open, snapdragons now come in double and open-face forms that no longer snap. Plants bear stalks of flowers in white, cream, yellow, burgundy, red, pink, orange, or bronze. Heights vary from 10 inches to 4 feet.

How to grow: Give plants full sun and rich, moist, well-drained soil. Sow seeds indoors, and transplant to the garden after the last spring frost date. Pinch young plants to encourage branching. Tall varieties need staking. Deadhead to encourage repeat bloom.

Uses: Use the tall selections for the back of the border and as cut flowers. Dwarf types are great as edging and in containers.

Related species and varieties: Many sizes and flower types are available in a range of colors. Select the height that suits your needs.

Snapdragons are prized for their columnar stateliness.

Hardiness: Zone 3

Description: Snowdrops bear dainty, 1-inch hanging flowers on 6-inch stems. The flowers are white with greenish inner petals. When grown in large masses, the combined fragrance perfumes the air. The leaves are strap-like or grassy, appearing with the flowers and fading away in late spring.

SNOWDROP
(Galanthus nivalis)
Type: Bulb

How to grow: Plant bulbs 3 inches deep and 3 inches apart in an area where they can grow undisturbed for many years. The plant is easily forced indoors. Snowdrops perform poorly in warm climates. Propagate by division.

Uses: Although they can be grown in beds and borders, snowdrops are best used for naturalizing. They adapt readily to lawns, meadows, and woods. Although their stems are rather short, they are popular cut flowers.

Related species and varieties: Flore Pleno is a double-flowered form of the common snowdrop. Giant snowdrop (*G. Elwesii*) is only slightly larger than its cousin and blooms later.

This plant is one of the first flowers of spring, blooming as early as January in the South and as late as April in the North. The flowers often push their way up through the snow.

STOKES' ASTER
(Stokesia laevis)

Type: Perennial

Hardiness: Zones 5 to 9

Description: Leaves are alternate and spiny-toothed toward the base, with the upper leaves clasping the stem. Fluffy blue to lavender flowers are 2 to 5 inches across on well-branched, 1- to 2- foot stems.

How to grow: *Stokesias* need full sun and good, well-drained soil. New plants take a year or two to settle in before maximum bloom. Wet winter soil is the main killer of these plants. In the northern part of their growing range (zone 5), Stokes' aster appreciates winter mulch. Remove spent blooms to encourage continued flowering through September.

Propagation: By seed or by division in spring

Uses: *Stokesias* are excellent decorative flowers for the front of the bed or border. They are good cut flowers, and the seedpods can be used in dried arrangements.

Stokes' aster, a native American wildflower that looks similar to a China aster, was originally found from South Carolina to Florida and Louisiana.

Description: These North American natives can be 15-foot-high giants or foot-tall dwarfs in containers. All bear showy daisy-type flowers with a broad central eye and yellow, gold, maroon, or creamy yellow petals. Many petals are bi-colored, and flowers can be single or double.

How to grow: Grow sunflowers in full sun and average, moist but well-drained soil. Plants tolerate heat and drought. Taller varieties may need staking.

Propagation: By seed. Sow seeds outdoors after the last spring frost date, or sow indoors for an early start. Seeds germinate in 10 to 15 days at 70° to 75°F.

Uses: Use dwarf types in beds and borders and taller selections at the back of borders or as a natural screen. Choose a multi-branched variety if you are growing sunflowers for cutting.

SUNFLOWER
(Helianthus annuus)

Type: Annual

Since sunflowers are heliotropic, their flower heads tend to turn and follow the path of the sun all day.

SWEET ALYSSUM
(Lobularia maritima)
Type: Annual

Description: Sweet alyssum bears clusters of tiny, fragrant flowers for months on end. Plants grow only a few inches high but spread as much as a foot in diameter. Although white is the most planted color, pink, lavender, and darker shades of violet are also available.

How to grow: Alyssum grows best in full sun in cool weather but tolerates partial shade. In mild climates, sow in fall for blooms in winter. Otherwise, sow seeds outdoors in spring as soon as the soil is no longer frozen, or sow seeds indoors 4 to 6 weeks earlier and move small plants to the garden. Seeds germinate in 7 to 14 days at 65° to 70°F.

Uses: Use alyssum for edging beds and borders, in rock gardens, or between paving stones.

Related varieties: 'Carpet of Snow' is a popular white variety. 'Royal Carpet' bears violet purple blooms. The Wonderland series consists of 'White,' 'Rosy-Red,' and 'Deep Purple.'

Sweet alyssum flowers for months, even through the winter in milder climates. A member of the mustard family, alyssum is quite fragrant.

In cool maritime or mountain climates, these natives of Italy will bring their beauty all summer. In zones 9 and 10, they're best in cool seasons, winter, and early spring.

SWEET PEA
(Lathyrus odoratus)
Type: Annual

Description: Sweet peas are vining plants that vigorously climb fences or other supports to a height of 6 or 8 feet. The flowers can be pink, white, red, lavender, or purple.

How to grow: Give sweet peas full sun and rich, moist, well-drained soil. They require cool weather. In areas with mild winters, grow them fall through winter. Elsewhere, sow seeds outdoors as soon as the soil has thawed and can be worked, or sow indoors in individual pots 4 to 6 weeks before that and transplant outside as early as possible. Pinch seedlings to encourage branching, and mulch plants to keep the soil cool. Seeds germinate in 10 to 14 days at 55° to 65°F.

Uses: Train sweet peas up and across fences and trellises. The dwarf varieties can be planted in the border. As cut flowers, sweet peas are superb.

TULIP
(*Tulipa* species)
Type: Bulb

Although tulips are associated with Holland, they actually are not native there; tulips descend mostly from species originating in the Middle East.

Darwin hybrid tulips are prized for their large flowers atop strong stems up to 30 inches tall.

Late spring Parrot tulips have feathery blooms atop 14- to 26-inch stems.

Kaufmanniana tulips resemble waterlilies and produce blooms on 6- to 12-inch stems.

Hardiness: Zones 3 to 8

Description: Tulips typically bear cup-shaped flowers in almost every shade but true blue. They can be double or single, fringed or twisted, perfumed or non-scented. The plants range in size from rock garden miniatures to 2½ feet or more in height. Most have broad leaves that quickly fade away in summer heat. Individual flowers last barely two weeks. However, since tulips offer various flowering seasons, you can have tulips in bloom from snow melt to the beginning of summer.

How to grow: Tulips may be grown as perennials or annuals. Plant bulbs 5 to 8 inches deep (less for tiny species tulips) and 4 to 6 inches apart in a sunny, well-drained area. Plant in fall, then water well. Divide bulbs every few years when flowering diminishes. Tulips need a period of cool weather to bloom. For that reason, pre-cooled bulbs are available for winter planting in warmer zones. These should be treated as annuals and replaced yearly.

Propagation: By division

Uses: Cut flowers, beds, and borders. Species tulips are ideal for naturalizing.

Related species and varieties: Tulips are organized into 15 divisions based on shape and origin. Tulips can also be grouped by bloom time (early, midseason, and late). Early blooming tulips include single early tulips (division 1), double early tulips (division 2), Kaufmanniana tulips (division 12), Fosteriana tulips (division 13), and Greigii tulips (division 14). Midseason tulips include medium-high Triumph (division 3) and the tall, giant-flowered Darwin hybrids (division 4). Late-season tulips include single late tulips (division 5), Lily-flowered tulips (division 6), fringed tulips (division 7), Viridiflora tulips (division 8), Parrot tulips (division 10), and double late tulips (division 11).

Versatile verbena comes in more than 250 annual and perennial varieties.

VERBENA
(Verbena × hybrida)
Type: Annual, perennial

Description: *Verbena x hybrida*, commonly called garden verbena, is a short-lived perennial that is usually grown as an annual. Trailing or mounding plants, verbenas range from 8 inches to 1 ½ feet tall. They are grown for their showy, rounded clusters of tiny trumpet-shaped flowers. Blooms come in violet, purple, rose, red, salmon-orange, or white.

How to grow: Give plants full sun and average or sandy, well-drained soil. Start from plants, or sow seeds indoors 12 to 14 weeks before the last spring frost date, and move plants to the garden after danger of frost has passed. Barely cover the seeds with soil, as darkness is necessary for germination. Germination takes 2 to 3 weeks at 65° to 75°F.

Uses: Use trailing types over walls and in rock gardens. Mounding cultivars are good for beds and borders.

Description: Also called Madagascar periwinkle, this heat-loving annual bears round, 5-petaled flowers in white, pink, pinkish red, lavender, or purple. Many blooms have a contrasting white eye.

How to grow: Give plants full sun and average to rich, well-drained soil. Plants thrive in heat and humidity. They are perennials in zone 10. Start with plants, or sow seeds indoors 3 to 4 months before the last spring frost date. Move to garden after all danger of frost has passed. Germination takes 14 to 21 days at 70° to 75°F. Cover seed, since darkness aids germination. Take root cuttings to overwinter plants, if desired.

VINCA
(Catharanthus roseus)
Type: Annual

Uses: Use vincas as edging or ground cover, or plant drifts of them in flower beds.

Hardiness: Zones 4 to 9

Description: Wisteria vines produce long strands of fragrant flowers, usually blue-violet, lavender, or mauve in color. Chinese wisteria (*Wisteria sinensis*) is a deciduous perennial vine that grows vigorously to 25 feet or more and features 6- to 12-inch-long clusters (racemes) of mildly-fragrant, blue-violet flowers. Japanese wisteria (*Wisteria floribunda*) typically grows 10 to 25 feet and features 18- to 36-inch-long drooping clusters of fragrant, violet, blue, pink, or white flowers. American wisteria (*Wisteria frutescens*) is a twining deciduous woody vine that grows to 40 feet or more and bears fragrant lilac-purple flowers on strands up to 6 inches long.

WISTERIA
(Wisteria species)
Type: Vine

This pergola frame is covered with Chinese wisteria (*Wisteria sinensis*). The vines of Chinese wisteria are extremely heavy, so supports must be strong.

Japanese wisteria (*Wisteria floribunda*) drip down from their stems like a violet waterfall.

Wisteria frutescens, American wisteria, is a counterclockwise twining vine native to the southeastern United States with late-spring, fragrant flowers of purple-blue or white.

How to grow: Chinese and Japanese wisteria vines are considered invasive in some areas of the United States, so American wisteria may be the best option for many gardeners. American wisteria also blooms faster. Plant wisteria in full sun in a rich, moist, well-drained soil. If the plant fails to flower after 5 years, dig into its root zone with a sharp shovel to root prune it (sometimes a sudden shock seems to get it going). Ordinary trellises are often crushed by the weight of this massive vine. Consider something more solid, like metal pipe.

Uses: Wisterias are great for patio coverage and growing over large structures. They can also be trained to tree form.

YARROW
(Achillea millefolium)

Type: Perennial

Hardiness: Zones 3 to 8

Description: Also called *achilleas*, yarrows grow 1 to 4 feet high, blooming from June until frost. Flowers are small and arranged in flat heads on top of stout stems. Blooms come in yellow, pink, apricot, red, white, or violet. The foliage is finely cut, with a ferny texture.

How to grow: Yarrows tolerate drought and are suitable for any garden soil that has good drainage. Plants perform best in full sun, although they will put up with a bit of shade. Propagate by division in spring or fall or by sowing seeds.

Uses: Yarrows are excellent in garden borders and in mass plantings.

Related varieties: Many hybrids are available in a range of rich colors. 'Summer Wine' bears pink buds that open to dark pink flowers on 2-foot-tall stems. 'Coronation Gold' bears deep yellow flowers.

Yarrow's Latin name means "a thousand leaves," a reference to the plant's fine, feathery foliage.

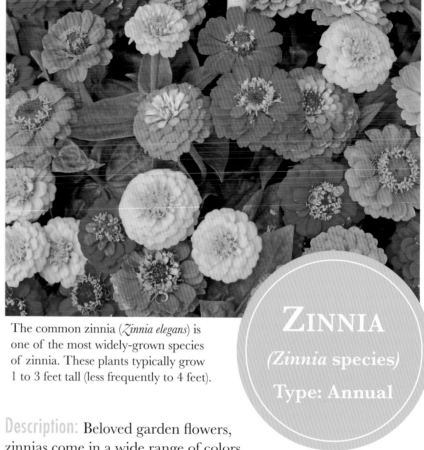

The common zinnia (*Zinnia elegans*) is one of the most widely-grown species of zinnia. These plants typically grow 1 to 3 feet tall (less frequently to 4 feet).

ZINNIA
(Zinnia **species***)*

Type: Annual

Description: Beloved garden flowers, zinnias come in a wide range of colors, sizes, and flower forms. Flowers may be single, semi-double, or double and range in width from 2 to 5 inches. Flowers come in red, yellow, pink, magenta, orange, white, or green. Heights vary from 6 inches to 4 feet.

How to grow: Give zinnias full sun and rich, well-drained soil. Powdery mildew can be a problem in humid weather. Sow seeds outdoors after the last spring frost date. Sow seeds indoors 4 weeks before that date for earlier bloom. Seeds germinate in 5 to 7 days at 70° to 75°F. Deadhead to prolong bloom.

Uses: Plant dwarf types as edging. Use taller zinnias with other annuals or in masses in beds and borders. Zinnias make excellent cut flowers.

Related varieties: Many colors and mixes are available. Profusion and Zahara series are disease-resistant plants.

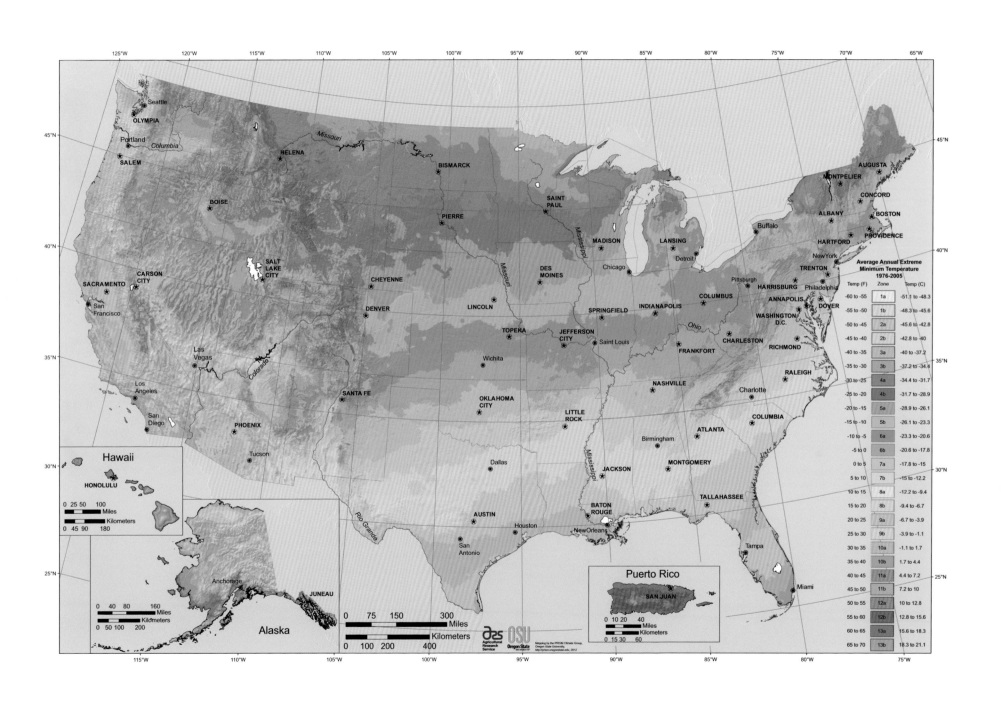

Temp (F)	Zone	Temp (C)
-60 to -55	1a	-51.1 to -48.3
-55 to -50	1b	-48.3 to -45.6
-50 to -45	2a	-45.6 to -42.8
-45 to -40	2b	-42.8 to -40
-40 to -35	3a	-40 to -37.2
-35 to -30	3b	-37.2 to -34.4
-30 to -25	4a	-34.4 to -31.7
-25 to -20	4b	-31.7 to -28.9
-20 to -15	5a	-28.9 to -26.1
-15 to -10	5b	-26.1 to -23.3
-10 to -5	6a	-23.3 to -20.6
-5 to 0	6b	-20.6 to -17.8
0 to 5	7a	-17.8 to -15
5 to 10	7b	-15 to -12.2
10 to 15	8a	-12.2 to -9.4
15 to 20	8b	-9.4 to -6.7
20 to 25	9a	-6.7 to -3.9
25 to 30	9b	-3.9 to -1.1
30 to 35	10a	-1.1 to 1.7
35 to 40	10b	1.7 to 4.4
40 to 45	11a	4.4 to 7.2
45 to 50	11b	7.2 to 10
50 to 55	12a	10 to 12.8
55 to 60	12b	12.8 to 15.6
60 to 65	13a	15.6 to 18.3
65 to 70	13b	18.3 to 21.1

Average Annual Extreme Minimum Temperature 1976-2005

Chapter 5
FLOWER ARRANGING

Like any work of art, a beautiful arrangement of cut flowers can brighten a room—and our spirits. Creating that work of art can be challenging, fun, and rewarding. The floral designer must not only pay attention to issues of style and color, but deal with the issues that come from working with living, changing plant material.

However, flower arranging doesn't need to be daunting. With a bit of practice, anyone can make an array of arrangements, from simple and cheerful to stylish and complex. Brighten your own home or give away bouquets as gifts to friends!

This chapter introduces some basic principles of arrangement and design before giving you step-by-step guidance in creating 11 unique arrangements. Get ideas for repurposing a grocery store bouquet (page 120), creating party favors for bridal showers (page 122), and developing both classic traditional arrangements and striking modern ones. The arrangements shown in this chapter will spur ideas for your own designs. As you experiment and incorporate your own ideas, you'll grow in confidence and get even more enjoyment from the process!

Supplies

Like any other creative project, arranging flowers is easier if all the necessary materials have been gathered together before you start. Since flowers are so perishable, the more quickly and efficiently each step is performed, the less the materials are handled, the longer the flowers—and your handiwork!—will last. Here is what you'll need to make most flower arrangements.

Floral Foam: Floral foam acts as a base in an arrangement, adding structure to foliage and flowers. Floral foam comes in different shapes and sizes. Most commonly, you'll see rectangular bricks. Check the label before you buy. A dry form of floral foam is available for silk arrangements, but wet floral foam should be used for live flowers. Soak floral foam in water (and flower preservative) before using it. Use a sharp knife to cut it down to the shape you need. Floral foam can be re-used if it's been soaked in water but not used. However, if your floral foam already has holes in it from stems, it's best to use a fresh piece of floral foam.

As with any arrangement, you'll need to add water to keep the arrangement fresh. Add water slowly to the arrangement, letting it soak into the foam.

Twine, Raffia, Rubber Bands and Jute: You can use raffia for several purposes: as a bow, or to bind stems together neatly. String, jute, and twine can also be used. See page 122, Party Favor, for an arrangement that uses jute to good purpose.

Floral Knife: A floral knife can be used to strip leaves and cut stems. Floral knives work especially well for soft, spongy stems like those of tulips (see page 124).

Floral Scissors and Snips: Use floral scissors and snips to prepare flowers and foliage and to remove thorns and leaves. Keep your floral scissors sharp; blunt blades will crush the stems. Some snips will be better for thicker stems, and some for thinner ones. Use branch cutters, which resemble garden pruners, for tough stems and woody branches.

Tape: Clear waterproof tape can be placed in a grid across the top of the container in order to provide support and structure to stems. Several arrangements shown in this chapter use clear tape. Always make sure that the surface to which you're attaching the tape is completely dry, or the tape may not adhere. Use green floral tape to attach floral foam to its container or conceal wired stems.

Floral Frogs or Kenzan: Floral frogs or kenzan look like pincushions, but with the pins facing upward. The pins are affixed to a flat disk or mat and are used to anchor and provide structure to stems.

Floral frogs have a series of pins that hold flowers in place.

Floral Wire: Floral wire is sold in different thicknesses, or gauges. Use floral wire to strengthen and lengthen stems. You can conceal the wire with green floral tape.

Water Tubes or Picks: Water tubes or picks are used to keep individual flowers fresh when their stems don't reach the water level or foam in your container. Water tubes have a rubberized cap that secures the stem and prevents water from leaking.

Marbles, Stones and Shells: Marbles, stones, shells, and pebbles can all be used in the base of the arrangement to anchor stems and provide visual interest. See page 136, Terrarium, for an arrangement that uses stones.

Flower Food: To extend the life of a flower arrangement, use flower food. You can purchase the same flower food you'd receive with a store-bought bouquet in larger quantities for your own homemade arrangements. This white powder contains a biocide to curb fungal growth, a nutrient to feed the flowers, and an acidifier to balance the water's pH.

CONDITIONING FLOWERS

Before you begin an arrangement, you'll need to prepare, or condition, your flowers and foliage. For best results start out with fresh material that has been well cared for.

- If you're getting flowers from your own garden, it's best to pick them in the morning.
- Cut the ends of each stem at a diagonal angle. This allows the plant to absorb water more easily. Make sure your tools are kept sharp and that you make a clean cut.
- Strip excess leaves and those that would remain below the water line.
- Let the flowers rest in warm water.

When you're ready to work on the arrangement itself, you'll take some additional steps with each flower or piece of greenery. Hold the flower up against the container to determine the desired height. Then cut the end of the stem to achieve that height. An angled cut allows for more water intake.

MAINTAINING ARRANGEMENTS

An arrangement that is properly maintained will last longer. Here are a few tips to keep your arrangement fresh for as long as possible:

- Make sure you use clean containers. Between periods of use, clean the container with bleach and then rinse it with water.
- Change the water in the container every few days.
- Recut the stem of any flower that begins to fade or wilt.
- Place the arrangement in a cool place and keep it out of direct sunlight.
- Remove elements that have passed their prime, which will help keep the rest of the arrangement fresh.
- Be careful of placing the flower arrangement near fresh fruit. Fruit gives off ethylene gas, which damages flowers.
- You might hear advice that you should add sugar or bleach to the water, but these tips are not proven to work and may even cause harm.

BASIC DESIGN ELEMENTS

As with cooking, many people start an arrangement by looking at someone else's "recipe." As people build confidence and knowledge, though, they begin to adapt recipes to their own tastes and to take in account the materials they have on hand. They may even begin to develop their own recipes! As you grow in confidence and create your own arrangements, here are some basic design considerations to keep in mind:

- Color
- Texture
- Container choice
- Size, shape, and proportion
- Movement

Texture

A delicate fern looks like it would be soft to the touch; green trick dianthus resembles a puffball; succulents look smooth and edgy. One of the joys of flower arranging is that you're working in three dimensions. Take advantage of that by including a variety of complementary textures in your arrangements.

Container Choice

The container you choose isn't just functional—it is another design element. Does the color of the container contrast or clash with that of the flowers? Does the style of the container—classic or modern—match the style of the arrangement?

Size, Shape and Proportion

The container or vase you use helps determine the height and width of the arrangement. You want to produce something that looks balanced. However, you also want one element (flowers or container) to dominate so that it draws the eye. A general rule of thumb is that if you have a vertical container, the height of the flowers should be about one and a half times taller than the height of the container.

Before you begin, you also want to think about where and how the arrangement will be used. A small bowl of daisies will look lovely on the coffee table but lonely on a long buffet. A tall arrangement of iris will cheer a dark foyer but hinder conversation at the dinner table.

Movement

As you work on an arrangement, step back every so often. What draws your eye? Ideally your design has a sense of movement that leads you through the arrangement, with a mix of large "hero" flowers that act as focal points and smaller "fill" flowers and foliage that add texture and depth. A variety in the size of the blooms and the shape of the flowers will keep your eyes moving.

Color Considerations

When selecting flowers, it's helpful to know a few basics about the color wheel and some harmonizing color schemes.

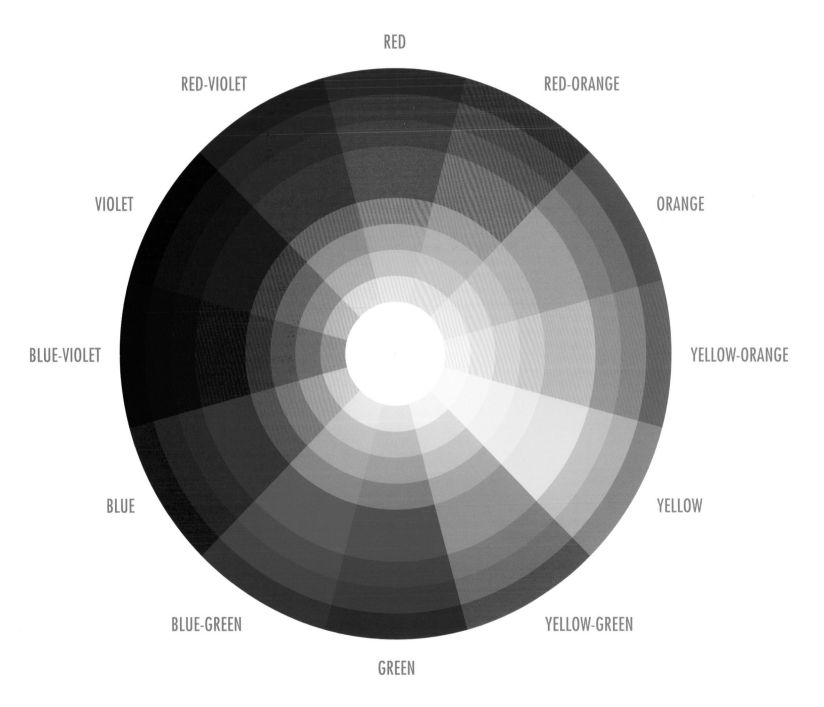

RED

RED-VIOLET

RED-ORANGE

VIOLET

ORANGE

BLUE-VIOLET

YELLOW-ORANGE

BLUE

YELLOW

BLUE-GREEN

YELLOW-GREEN

GREEN

Monochromatic

Monochromatic color schemes are based on one color. They use variations in value (lightness or darkness) and intensity (brightness or dullness) of a single color.

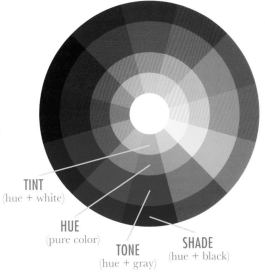

TINT
(hue + white)

HUE
(pure color)

TONE
(hue + gray)

SHADE
(hue + black)

Complementary

Complementary color schemes use two colors that are directly opposite of each other on the color wheel (e.g., orange and blue; red and green). This scheme contrasts a warm color (yellow, yellow-orange, orange, red-orange, red, or red-violet) with a cool color (violet, blue-violet, blue, blue-green, green, or yellow-green).

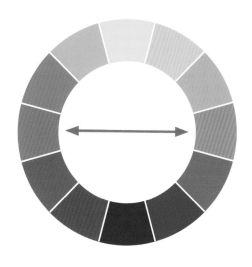

Analogous

Analogous color schemes use colors that are adjacent to each other on the color wheel (e.g., blue-violet, blue, blue-green). While similar to monochromatic schemes, analogous schemes offer more nuances. Typically one color is chosen as a dominant color and the others are used as accent colors.

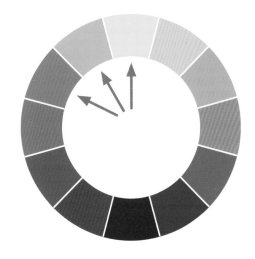

Triadic

Triadic color schemes use three colors equally spaced around the color wheel (e.g., orange, green, and violet; red-orange, blue-violet, and yellow-green). On a twelve-color wheel, selecting every fourth color on the wheel would make a triadic scheme.

HERE ARE SOME BASIC DESIGN PRINCIPLES TO KEEP IN MIND:

- In flower design, green is treated as a neutral color.
- In a complementary arrangement, in order to draw the eye, one color should be dominant. The other color acts as an accent color.
- How does the color of the vase or container work with your choices?

VASE ASSORTMENT

YOU'LL NEED:

- Several small bud vases and jars
- Eucalyptus
- Asparagus fern (any fern can be used)
- Lavender
- Aster
- Lisianthus (both solid purple and variegated)
- Clematis
- Larkspur (snapdragon can substitute)

Create a versatile, stylish arrangement by using an assortment of small bud vases and jars, each filled with just a few flowers or pieces of greenery. Use a variety of heights and shapes to form an attractive grouping. This arrangement uses clear vases, but you can get a beautiful, harmonious effect by using vases in the same part of the color wheel as well.

Creating an arrangement with multiple containers is a great way to repurpose a grocery store bouquet. It's also a great way to use different flowers from your own garden. You can rotate flowers and foliage in and out of the arrangement for an ever-changing, long-lasting display.

This arrangement is unified by the color of the flowers, all shapes of purple. There is an array of different textures, from the softness of the asparagus fern (*asparagus plumosa*) to the silkiness of the lisianthus. Lavender and eucalyptus both add a subtle, attractive fragrance. The elements used are all easily available year-round. If you refresh the water as needed, the arrangement can last up to a week.

1. Gather your plants and containers. Fill the jars with water.

2. Here and as a general rule, begin by placing the greenery, which grounds and supports the arrangement. Hold each stem against the container to get an idea of the desired height, then snip the stem.

3. Remove any leaves that would be inside of the vase, underneath the water line. Not only does this create a neater look for the arrangement, but it also helps the arrangement last longer. Leaves in standing water rot more quickly.

4. Once your greenery is placed, begin placing your flowers.

5. You will find that sometimes your plants will naturally lean in one direction or the other. Find a way to place the plant so that it can follow its natural shape.

6. Rearrange the bottles and add and rearrange flowers and greenery until you love the result. Don't be afraid to remove an element that isn't working!

PARTY FAVOR

YOU'LL NEED:

- Mason jars
- Raffia or jute
- Fuschia spray roses
- Light pink spray roses
- White carnations

Depending on the different sizes and heights of your jars, consider adding larkspur, snapdragon, or delphinium as a vertical element.

If you're throwing a bridal shower or baby shower, decorate with groups of Mason jars filled with flowers. Mason jars are easy to find and inexpensive, and you can then send the jars home as party favors. The arrangement shown here uses traditional romantic colors, pinks and reds. You can also use the colors of the wedding party.

Use raffia, jute, or twine (available at craft stores) to tie together the stems. Tying the stems together gives the flowers structure in the wide-mouthed mason jars.

The flowers used here, white carnations and spray roses, are easy to acquire and available throughout the year. Bought new and maintained well, the arrangement will last about a week, perhaps even two.

1. Gather your containers and raffia or jute. Fill the jars with water.

2. Gather the carnations together, strip the stems of leaves, and measure the bunch against the height of the jar. Tie the stems together.

3. Cut the stems directly beneath the tie.

4. Grouped together, the carnations look almost like one large flower!

5. Gather your next bunch of flowers. Strip the stems of leaves.

6. Tie together the stems, cut them to the desired height, and place the flowers in water. Do the same for the remaining jars.

TULIPS

Though available throughout the year, tulips come into season in spring and make a great Mother's Day bouquet. Tulips come in many different colors, so choose your mom's favorite! Tulips have beautiful thick, green stems that display well in a clear vase.

Clear waterproof tape, available at craft stories, is placed in a grid over the top of the vase in order to provide structure to the stems. When using clear tape, make sure the surface to which you're applying the tape is dry. The tape won't adhere well to damp surfaces, although it can withstand moisture once applied.

Work with the natural bend and direction of the stems. Expect that a tulip arrangement will change over time—not only are tulips very responsive to sunlight, but they will continue to grow even after they're cut.

Tulips generally last a week or more, especially if they are still closed when purchased or cut. They'll last longer if they're kept in a cool room, out of direct sunlight.

1. Gather your tulips, a clear vase with water, and clear waterproof tape.

2. Use the tape to create a grid across the top of the vase.

3. Remove the leaves that would be below the water line. Tulip leaves can be stubborn, and their spongy stems are crushed easily, so use a floral knife for the cleanest cut.

4. Hold each tulip against the container to determine its desired height.

5. Cut the stem to that height using a floral knife. Watch out for crushed stems, which will get soft and moldy.

6. Prepare each tulip and place it in the vase. If the stem bends, follow the natural direction of the stem in placing it.

Monochromatic

This simple but elegant monochromatic arrangement uses flowers in different shades and tints of the same section of the color wheel. The greenery used, dusty miller, adds texture and depth.

The elements used here are available year around. Both roses and dusty miller are popular garden plants.

If you develop this arrangement when the roses are tight, they will open over time for a beautiful bouquet that can last up to 7 to 10 days.

1. Gather a simple vase and clear waterproof tape. Fill the vase with water, making sure the lid is completely dry.

2. Use the tape to create a grid across the top of the vase that will anchor the arrangement.

3. Prepare and add the dusty miller.

4. Prepare and add the roses. Leaves above the lid of the vase can be left on for extra texture and structure.

YOU'LL NEED:

- Fishbowl-shaped container
- Clematis in different colors
- Clear tape

Clematis, a member of the buttercup family, is a popular garden plant. Different varieties in many colors bloom through the summer months and into September. This arrangement uses three shades of purple clematis to create an informal arrangement that will brighten an entryway or kitchen table.

The round fishbowl container lends itself well to an arrangement that can be viewed from all angles. As you work, make sure you turn the container to ensure that the flowers and stems are spaced evenly.

Clematis has thin stems, so this arrangement uses clear tape in a tight grid to add structure. You can use ivy or the plant's own extra stems and leaves to add additional support and structure to the arrangement.

1. Gather bunches of clematis in the desired color, a round container filled with water, and clear tape. A floral frog can be used instead of tape.

2. Apply the tape in a tight grid. The grid spaces are smaller than in the Tulips arrangement (page 124) because the stems are thinner. Add tape along diagonal lines.

3. Measure the stems and cut them to the desired height. Peel away extra leaves. You can use the stems and leaves you strip off as added greenery.

4. Continue to add flowers and stems to fill in the grid. As you work, consider the arrangement from all angles.

VERTICAL ARRANGEMENT

YOU'LL NEED:

- Low, horizontal container
- Floral foam
- Leatherleaf fern
- Asparagus fern
- Palm branch
- Snakegrass
- Dendrobium orchid
- Hydrangea
- Green trick dianthus

This dramatic vertical arrangement uses tropical plants for an eye-catching result. Purple orchids rise against a backdrop of snakegrass and palm branch, while hydrangea and green trick dianthus add texture at the base.

Tropical plants are available throughout the year, but they may be more difficult to source than some of the other flowers and foliage used in this chapter. You'll most likely have to visit a florist's shop or a floral market. Potted orchids can be bought at a home improvement store.

Bamboo can be substituted for snakegrass. Liatris is a beautiful substitute for orchid.

1. Place saturated floral foam in your container. Depending on the heaviness of the container, you may want to tape your floral foam down with green floral tape to attach it securely.

2. With a vertical arrangement, develop the vertical element first. Begin with the tallest element, the snakegrass. Cut the snakegrass to the desired height.

3. Add the palm branch behind the snakegrass.

5. Begin to cover the floral foam with the base elements, the hydrangea and dianthus. The leaves can be left on, as they help cover the foam. Fill in the space and cover the lip of the container with ferns.

4. Orchids often come in water tubes. Gently remove them and add the orchids. Massage the orchid stems to create a gentle curve.

Contrasting Colors

YOU'LL NEED:

- Square container
- Floral foam
- Leatherleaf fern
- Tulips
- Asters
- Lisianthus
- Hypericum berry
- Wax flowers

Bright yellow and vibrant purple complement each other in this cheerful arrangement. (Yellow and violet are complementary colors appearing opposite each other on the color wheel.) Tulips, as the larger flowers with thicker stems, provide the base. The softer purple flowers act as an accent. Berries add texture.

The flowers in this arrangement are easily available. Purple hyacinth can be used in place of lisianthus and aster; however, hyacinth has limited seasonal availability.

Properly maintained, the arrangement can last about 5 to 7 days. It would make a great hostess gift or pick-me-up for a friend!

1. Select a square container.

2. Gather your plant materials. Cut a piece of saturated floral foam that fits the container.

3. Build a base of greenery with the leatherleaf fern.

4. Prepare and add your dominant flowers, the tulips. Space them evenly in the foam.

5. Fill in with the purple accent flowers, aster and lisianthus.

6. Add in the hypericum berry (shown above) and the wax flowers (see the final arrangement) as filler.

CLASSIC URN

YOU'LL NEED:

- Classic urn
- Floral foam
- Eucalyptus
- Leatherleaf fern
- Ivy
- Snapdragon
- Lace hydrangea
- White roses
- Peach roses

This traditional three-quarter arrangement is great for a vestibule or side table, where it will be placed against a wall. With a three-quarter arrangement, start building in the back of the arrangement, placing the tallest elements first. In this case, snapdragon adds a wonderful vertical element. The larger roses draw the eye.

When you place the arrangement, check that you can't see the wall through gaps.

The round container adds a classical touch; you can find similar containers at yard sales or in antique shops.

The arrangement is anchored in floral foam. In this case sections were cut and shaped from rectangular blocks; however, foam is also available in spheres.

1. Fit blocks of saturated floral foam to the container.

2. Begin placing the leatherleaf fern and eucalyptus. Start at the back of the arrangement instead of in the center.

3. Add snapdragon, the tallest of the flowers. Follow the natural curve of the snapdragon as you place it.

4. Fill in the arrangement with the hydrangea and roses. Take any discolored or wilted guard petals off the roses before you place them.

5. Fill in the rest of the arrangement. Add ivy, trailing downwards, in the front.

TERRARIUM

A terrarium-style container is a great way to display long-lasting succulents on a bed of pebbles or stones. As well as adding texture and beauty, the rocks elevate the succulents, keeping them alive. Succulents do not do well when placed directly on glass or when submerged in water.

Succulents pair extremely well with orchids. In this arrangement, the orchid adds a vertical element and a splash of color. While orchids are more expensive than many flowers, they catch the eye with their elegance and beauty.

A tall cylindrical container can be purchased wholesale or at a craft store. Succulents can be found in the flower section at a grocery store or garden center. If orchids are not available through your local supermarket, see your local florist, use a silk version, or buy a potted orchid plant at a home improvement store.

Refresh the water as necessary; you'll need to refresh the water more frequently if the arrangement is kept in sunlight. If necessary, remove any blooms that begin to wilt. Re-cut the orchid's stem to extend its life. If tended well, this arrangement could last at least a month.

1. Gather some succulents, an orchid, stones, and a tall cylindrical vase.

3. Add water to coat the rocks. Cut the orchid stem to an appropriate height and place it in the rocks.

2. Place the rocks in the bottom of the container. Rest the succulent or succulents on top.

OMBRÉ

In an ombré arrangement, the color gradually shades from dark to light. You can create an ombré arrangement in many different color palettes, although blue may prove difficult as there aren't as many blue flowers.

This fulsome arrangement has a lot of texture and depth. The long, low horizontal container makes it perfect for a table centerpiece or a mantle. While you work, look at the arrangement from many different angles, including from above.

The flowers and greens are anchored in floral foam, available in craft stores. Before floral foam is used, it needs to be submerged in water until it's fully saturated. Allow at least 10 minutes for this process, although floral foam can be left in water for a longer period of time without damage. Use a sharp knife to cut floral foam into the necessary shape. A floral knife can be used, but a kitchen knife with a longer blade may be easier to work with.

As you'll see, the floral foam doesn't have to be lower than the edge of the container, and in fact it may provide more structure and be easier to work with if it's just a little bit taller than the container. Greenery is used to camouflage the floral foam.

With water, this arrangement may last up to 5 to 7 days. Pour water in slowly and let it saturate the foam.

YOU'LL NEED:

- Low, horizontal container
- Floral foam
- Leatherleaf fern
- Lisianthus
- Asters
- Dahlias
- Roses
  (different sizes and colors)
- Carnations

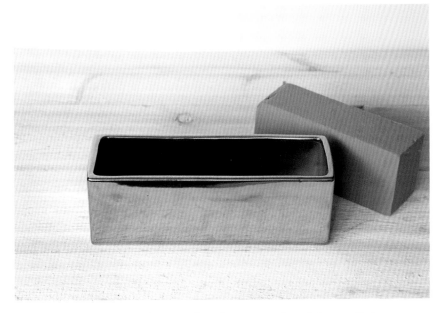

1. Select your container and gather your floral foam. Submerge the floral foam in water until it is fully saturated.

2. Fit the floral foam to the container. This container uses one block of floral foam and a section cut off from another block.

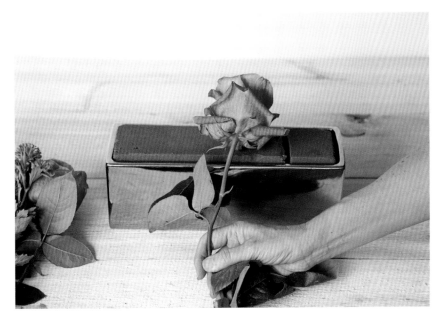

3. Large full-head roses have guard petals that can become wilted or discolored. Strip away these guard petals.

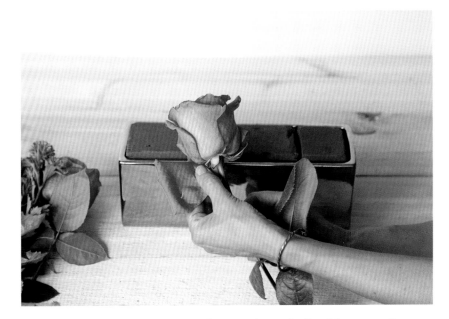

4. There are usually four to six guard petals. In this case a few other petals were also removed to make the roses more uniform in size.

5. Prepare the flowers by removing leaves and guard petals and cutting stems to the desired height. Begin by placing the greenery. This arrangement uses leatherleaf fern.

6. Starting with the dark colors, begin to fill in the arrangement. For variation within the same part of the color spectrum, incorporate different sizes and textures.

7. Ease the transition to a lighter shade by mixing in one or two flowers of the darker shade.

8. Continue filling in the arrangement. View the arrangement from multiple angles as you work.

ASYMMETRICAL

YOU'LL NEED:

- Clear, square container
- Clear waterproof tape or floral foam
- Floral wire
- Glue tabs
- Bear grass
- Tropical leaves
- Sedum (two colors)

Asymmetry is the key to the modern look of this arrangement. Curved leaves and grasses are not only visually compelling, but fun materials with which to work!

The clear, square container is lined with tropical leaves that add visual interest. Tropical leaves are the exception to the general rule against putting leaves under the water line, as they're very strong and water resistant. Leaves from the Ti plant are used here; leaves from the *Aspidistra* family would also work well.

In this case a grid is made with clear tape to support the structure of the arrangement. However, floral foam would also work, as long as the leaves are large enough to conceal it.

1. Gather the container and two tropical leaves. If necessary, trim the leaves down to size to fit in the container.

2. Line the container with the leaves. Fill the container with water.

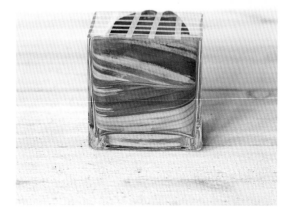

3. Making sure the lip of the container is completely dry, use clear waterproof tape to create a grid.

4. Gather five or six stems of bear grass. Bind one end with floral wire.

5. Bind the other end with floral wire.

6. Create a loop with the bear grass. Bind the ends of the loop together.

7. Place the bear grass in the container. You may need to remove some tape pieces from the grid to fit the bear grass.

8. Using a glue tab for security, roll a tropical leaf into itself.

9. Place the tropical leaf into the container.

11. Roll a second tropical leaf as you did in step 8 and secure it with a glue tab. Place the second rolled leaf in the back of the container.

10. Place the sedum in the container, clustering the colors together.